The Media Diet for Kids

The Media Diet for Kids

A Parent's Survival Guide to TV and Computer Games

Teresa Orange & Louise O'Flynn

HAY HOUSE

Australia • Canada • Hong Kong
South Africa • United Kingdom • United States

Published and distributed in the United Kingdom by Hay House UK Ltd, Unit 62, Canalot Studios, 222 Kensal Rd, London W10 5BN. Tel.: (44) 20 8962 1230; Fax: (44) 20 8962 1239. www.hayhouse.co.uk

Published and distributed in the United States of America by Hay House, Inc., PO Box 5100, Carlsbad, CA 92018-5100. Tel.: (1) 760 431 7695 or (800) 654 5126; Fax: (1) 760 431 6948 or (800) 650 5115. www.hayhouse.com

Published and distributed in Australia by Hay House Australia Ltd, 18/36 Ralph St, Alexandria NSW 2015. Tel.: (61) 2 9669 4299; Fax: (61) 2 9669 4144. www.hayhouse.com.au

Published and distributed in the Republic of South Africa by Hay House SA (Pty), Ltd, PO Box 990, Witkoppen 2068. Tel./Fax: (27)11 706 6612. orders@psdprom.co.za

Distributed in Canada by Raincoast, 9050 Shaughnessy St, Vancouver, BC V6P 6E5. Tel.: (1) 604 323 7100; Fax: (1) 604 323 2600

© Teresa Orange and Louise O'Flynn, 2005

Design: Julie Martin • *Illustrations:* Mat Pilbeam

A catalogue record for this book is available from the British Library.

ISBN 1-4019-0768-7

Composition by Scribe Design Ltd, Ashford, Kent, UK.

Printed and bound in Great Britain by The Cromwell Press Ltd, Trowbridge, Wilts.

To mum and dad

Just five more minutes, pleeese!

Foreword

You hear it all the time, don't you? 'Children these days have so much choice.' And they have too, and that's fine. Choice can be hugely enriching, but it can be overwhelming.

Thinking back to my own childhood, we could either listen to the radio (one programme), read books (Blyton mostly) or play out. That was it. Now they have in-house entertainment of every conceivable variety, and all instantly available, instantly stimulating. Like fast food, it is seductive and compelling, and can become deeply habit-forming. Like fast food, too much of it is seriously bad for you. We know that.

The question is then how you as a parent can find the positive in all this, so that your child can benefit from the best of it rather than suffer from the worst of it, or from simple overindulgence.

Never has parenting been so complex as it is now. This much-needed book helps parents to unravel these complexities, giving so much confidence to them in their efforts to ration and select, in their attempts to help children towards making sensible choices for themselves.

Like all diets, it is very difficult to keep at first, but like all diets once the new habits have been inculcated and accepted, the need and the appetite diminish, and it all becomes so much easier and happier for child and parent alike.

Michael Morpurgo
Children's Laureate 2003-2005

Thank You

When we started this project, neither of us had any idea how big it would become and just how many people would get involved.

We would like to thank everyone who has helped us with our research. Friends and strangers. Grandparents and parents. Kids and carers. Teachers and professional experts. We hope the book does justice to your many and varied contributions.

We owe a big thanks to Michelle, Jo, Meg, Giovanna and Leanne at Hay House – not only for taking us on – but for their professional guidance and support. Thanks also to our agent, Robert, for making the whole thing possible; our editor, Louise, for knocking our words into shape; Mat, our illustrator, for bringing those words so vividly to life, and to Julie and Steve on the design team.

A special mention needs to be made to mum and dad for their tireless enthusiasm and encouragement, and to Simon for giving us the courage to pursue a gem of an idea.

None of this would have been possible without 'The Home Team' – Isabel, Christopher, Hugo, Ophelia and Alice. The book owes much of its character and contents to you – and, of course, without your screen appetite we would never have been inspired to take action in the first place.

Finally, a big hug and kisses to Andrew and Giles. Thanks for bearing with us and for being there every step of the way.

Calling all parents with screen-hungry kids!

This book is all about getting the balance right

Menu

INGREDIENTS

WHO IS THE DIET FOR?

It's a diet for screen-hungry kids ...

New evidence confirms our children are watching too much media - they're damaging themselves by bingeing on TV and computer games

This book helps parents know WHEN and HOW to say 'NO!

Just five more minutes, pleeese!

More specifically, IT'S A DIET FOR TODDLERS TO TWELVE YEAR OLDS ...

because it's important to establish good media habits before the teenage years

WHAT IS THE MEDIA DIET?

A 3-step media consumption plan

Step 1: From calorie counting to time counting
- limiting the time your child spends in front of the TV or computer games

Step 2: From junk programming to healthy media
- ensuring your child's screen time is quality time

Step 3: From media addiction to media substitutes
- balancing the role media plays in your child's life

WHAT DOES THE DIET PROMISE?

It gives practical advice to stop 'media bingeing' and establish a healthy media balance

The result is a well-balanced media child – able to control the role of media in his or her teenage years

THE MEDIA DIET FOR KIDS TOOLKIT

For copies of any of the charts visit www.mediadietforkids.com

Calling all parents with screen-hungry kids!

Just five more minutes, pleeese!

Most parents will be familiar with the situation ... the kids are glued to the telly or gripped by some new computer game. There's homework to be done and it's time for bed. But they're there. In front of *that* screen.

'Turn *that* thing off!' you shout.

'Just five more minutes, pleeese!' they reply.

You reluctantly give way ... and before you know it, another half an hour has passed.

As parents, most of us have firm views about bringing up our children. We naturally want the best for them. We care about the food they eat, the friends they make, how they behave and what they're taught at school. So, we'll make them eat their greens. We'll take a special interest in their new friends at school. We'll be quick to tick them off if they don't say 'please' or 'thank you'. And we'll nag them as much as is needed to get their homework done.

Why is it, then, that we don't have a clearer idea about how to deal with two of the biggest single influences in our children's lives – the TV and computer? Perhaps it's because we don't appreciate just how much time kids do spend watching TV or playing on the computer, and the harm that it might be doing them.

Believe it or not, eleven to fifteen year olds spend on average 53 hours a week in front of the screen – whether it's watching TV, videos or DVDs, playing computer games or just being online. This compares with 38 hours a week in 1994. It means that many kids are now spending more than seven and a half hours in front of the screen every day. And the majority of children spend more time watching TV than actually learning at school.[1]

1

Increasing Screen Consumption

Average number of hours per week* amongst 11–15 year olds

	1994	1997	2000	2004**
TV	26.6	27.3	33.5	32.1
Videos/DVDs	5.9	5.7	5.8	5.4
Computer Games	5.8	5.9	7.3	7.7
Internet			5.2	7.3
TOTAL 'Screen Time'	38.3	38.9	51.8	52.5

*Averages per week include time spent in school holidays and at school
**2004 average internet usage comprises 4.2 hours at home, 1.7 hours at school, 1.4 hours elsewhere

Source: Youth TGI, Copyright BMRB International 1994-2004

Just five more minutes, pleeese!

Most people would agree this can't be a good thing. And now there is evidence to prove it isn't. How to control the TV and computer games has become a major challenge of parenting today. Even those parents who are coping seem to find it increasingly difficult.

It's time to introduce ourselves ...

We're Teresa and Louise, two experienced media professionals. Here's where we're coming from:

Teresa says:

'I have a degree in psychology, and have always been interested in how children behave and think. I was the children's expert at the advertising giant, J Walter

Thompson, and worked on some of the most well-known children's advertising campaigns. These included, amongst others, campaigns for My Little Pony, Smarties, Tony the Tiger and Snap Crackle Pop.

I then set up my own children's media research company, and have worked with large companies such as Kellogg's, Kraft and K'Nex to develop and market children's brands and products.'

Louise says:

'I have also had a career in the media – but in public relations. Like advertising, good PR is about influencing people. You're either trying to get them to think a certain thing, or buy a particular product. And again, the way you do it is by exploiting the media.

I was responsible for promoting the UK's biggest consumer brand – The National Lottery. We used the media – in all its different shapes and forms – to tap into the emotions and desires of people who wanted to become millionaires overnight. Two areas that were of particular concern, however, were gambling addiction and the protection of under-age children. I became heavily involved in both these issues, developing strategies to help protect those who are most vulnerable from the temptations of gambling.'

As well as media professionals, we're also two mums with screen-hungry kids. We know just how difficult it is to control the use of the screen at home. Between the two of us we have five children – boys and girls – ranging from two to twelve years old.

We share our children's great love for all things media. We're media enthusiasts ourselves. We had a niggling feeling, however, that things weren't quite right. We were worried about the balance in their lives. Perhaps they were becoming too glued to the screen.

So we started to ask ourselves some questions:

• How much time should our children be spending in front of the screen?
• What's the best way of controlling their media consumption?
• What other things should we be encouraging them to do?

Our Home Team

Alice aged 2 – *favourites:*
TV: Milkshake *Video:* Bob The Builder

Ophelia aged 3 – *favourites:*
TV: CBeebies *Video:* Finding Nemo

Hugo aged 6 – *favourites:*
TV: Tracy Beaker *DVD:* Ice Age *Computer Game:* FIFA 2005

Christopher aged 9 – *favourites:*
TV: The Simpsons *Computer Games:* Medal of Honour (by myself);
RollerCoaster Tycoon (with my sister)

Isabel aged 12 – *favourites:*
TV: Films *Computer Games:* Sims (by myself); RollerCoaster Tycoon (with my
brother)

Our kids – a bunch of media enthusiasts

Why we're taking action ...

We started writing this book because we realised we weren't the only mums like us around. Lots of us – and dads, of course – have children with big screen appetites. That's modern living.

As media professionals we know how the media works and are familiar with the tricks of the trade. We know, for instance, how to grab and keep a child's attention. And as a child researcher, Teresa understands what makes children tick and how to get inside their minds. We wanted to put this expertise to good use. So, we decided to use what we had learnt in our media lives to explore how parents could control, and make the most of, the media when bringing up children. As one friend put it, we've turned from poachers to gamekeepers.

We also became aware of the growing number of new research studies that show children suffer long-term problems if they spend too much time in front of the TV, or computer screen, in their formative years. These latest studies are important because they've followed children closely from early childhood to adulthood. And, rather than being experiments carried out in some laboratory setting, these studies have actually monitored children growing up in their own home environment.

Scrambled brains and couch potatoes are only part of the problem. In fact, there are a whole range of physical, social and mental conditions that millions of children are suffering, simply because they're spending so much time watching TV or playing on the computer. And most children – whether their parents realise it or not – are affected.

Research shows that more than two hours a day in front of the television can cause long-term damage. So, no longer is it just a gut feeling we might have, that too much screen time is bad for our children. There's now real proof that if we over-indulge our children with modern media, we may be damaging them for life.

IT'S TIME FOR A DIET:

Bingeing on screen time – whether TV, DVDs, videos, computer games, mobile games (e.g. Game Boy) or online games – is bad for your kid's health

 It's time to get the balance right

How we did our research – who we talked to

We decided to do our own research and interviewed over 100 people with first-hand experience of bringing up children – mums, dads, grandparents, carers, teachers, children and media experts. They came from a range of different backgrounds. Some lived in the city, others in the country. All of them had a wealth of different views and experiences.

We didn't just look at the problems of media bingeing. We wanted, above all, to explore the solutions. What strategies did parents have for controlling modern media in their children's lives? Did they have any good tips for 'switching off' or monitoring content? What activities away from the screen did they think should be encouraged? And, in a world where we constantly seem short of time, is there an easy solution for time-pressed parents?

OUR RESEARCH

Discussion Groups:

with mums, dads, carers, grandparents ... and kids themselves!

One-to-one Chats:

with children, single parents, families experiencing difficulties and parents with problem kids

Expert Interviews:

with teachers, psychologists, play experts and media professionals

 Over 100 people helped us write this book

The findings were revealing. There was widespread enthusiasm for the wonders of modern media, but also concern that kids were becoming too dependent on it. There was also a feeling of frustration and helplessness.

Most parents didn't have an overall 'strategy' and there was no general policy for setting limits. It tended to be haphazard: 'Help, you've been in front of the computer far too long – turn it off!' The vast majority of parents wanted some help and guidance.

And we talked to the kids too ...

The kids wanted guidance too. Most of the kids we interviewed sensed that too much screen time is a bad thing. They were looking to their parents to take the lead. As one eleven year old boy said, 'If you don't get told to come off, it's hard to know when to come off.'

And kids whose parents did take firm action generally seemed to welcome it. 'I don't like it if I'm glued in front of the telly,' one ten year old boy told us. 'We have rough guidelines and it kind of helps you. We've got into the habit of living to them.'

One of the most revealing things was what children said when they were asked how they would react, as parents, if their kids became media bingers. These were all words they used to describe their feelings: Upset. Guilty. Annoyed. Cross. Most kids – apart from the serious media bingers – thought their parents were far too weak. 'They say "no" and don't mean it' was a frequent comment. They were also determined that if they had children, they would be stricter and do more to control the screen at home.

What kids say ...

About their parents ...

'My parents always miss things like the news because we're on the PlayStation and then they get angry. They should be firmer, but I'm not telling mum that.'   *11 year old boy*

About how they would feel if they had media bingeing kids ...

'I would be upset with them. I would want them to go outside and enjoy that, rather than just sitting in front of the TV. I would feel it was my fault, because that's how I've brought them up.'   *12 year old girl*

About how they would bring up kids ...

66 'I'd let them have two and a half hours in the afternoon on the computer, and two hours on the telly, on a home day. And on a week day, an hour on the PlayStation and an hour on the telly.' *12 year old boy*

66 'I'd tell them to get something else in their lives.' *12 year old boy*

And that's how The Media Diet for Kids came about. Not only did it seem to us that parents wanted to be able to take firmer control – kids wanted them to be firmer too.

So, it's time to take action

We came across several parents who had been slow to act. They had been happy to let their kids spend hours and hours watching TV or playing on the computer. Then something snapped. They couldn't stand it any more. The only way they could deal with the problem was by getting rid of the TV and computer altogether.

These kids quickly went from one extreme to another – from media bingeing to media starvation. They were suddenly deprived of all the advantages that modern media has to offer. And that's not a good thing for anyone.

The Media Diet for Kids provides a simple and practical solution to getting balance in our children's lives. There's no great science to it. A lot of it is just common sense. In the same way as we're told to encourage our kids to eat five pieces of fruit and vegetable a day, the diet recommends a mix of activities for our children.

The diet is for toddlers to twelve year olds. It provides parents with a three-step solution for controlling, and making the most of, TV and computer games. The end result will be a well-balanced media child, able to control the role of media in his or her teenage years.

It's a positive approach because we believe modern media should be an important part of family life. The diet isn't, therefore, just about cutting down on media consumption. It looks at how to make media time quality time, and how to encourage a healthy mix of activities away from the screen.

9

This is our book. But it also belongs to all the people we've talked to over the past year. The pages are full of their tips and advice – as well as their concerns and frustrations.

So, calling all parents with screen-hungry kids ... it's time to read on. We hope you enjoy reading the book, and above all, that it encourages you – and gives you the confidence – to take action.

I'm ready to take action ... are you?

Part 1

Why it's all about balance

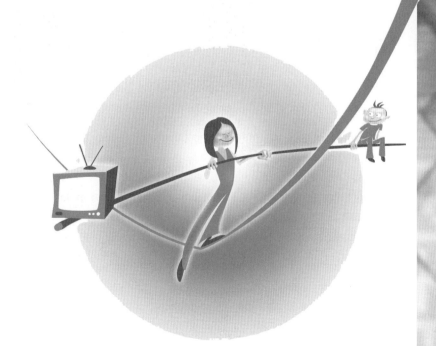

THE NEED FOR BALANCE

- Looking at media opportunities
- Recognising media dangers

Turn it off!

A mum who knows the facts and has the confidence to act

In order to persuade your child to follow The Media Diet – and get your partner's support – everyone has to understand the need to take action.

We spoke to one single mum who was concerned she was losing her twelve year old daughter to the computer. Every evening her daughter spent five hours on it, and so they would rarely have time together. She described her dilemma. She wanted to get her away from the screen but she was in two minds about it. Was it for her daughter's sake, or her own sake, that she wanted her to stop? If she was enjoying herself so much on the computer, was it really *that* damaging?

This section provides her – and any parent unsure about the need to take action – with the reasons why a healthy media balance is so important. First, we look at all the positive things your child gets from the media and then we look at the dangers.

Chapter 1

Media opportunities – why every parent should include media on the menu

SO MUCH TO OFFER ... CAN'T BE WITHOUT IT!

- Entertainment
- Relaxation
- Education
- Social Opportunities
- Fuels Interests
- Encourages Creativity
- IT Literacy
- Independence

Can't do without it – got to be part of it!

Let's start with the positive.

We're living through a media revolution. We all want to be part of it. It's only natural. Time and time again, when we spoke to parents – particularly the dads – their eyes lit up when they described the things their children were able to do because of the TV and computers.

One dad we spoke to, summed it up when he said:

> 'It's the future, isn't it? A child who hasn't got a computer won't learn eye and hand coordination. They won't know about the things which are so important later on. They'll be behind.'
>
> *Peter, dad of a boy and a girl, local council worker*

And he's right, of course. Our research highlighted eight specific areas where people felt that modern media plays a particularly positive role in children's development.

Entertainment

When we asked kids what they thought was the best thing about the screen, the answer was 'it's a boredom buster'. In other words, it's great entertainment.

We asked a group of eight and nine year old children to imagine life without screens. We wanted them to imagine that they woke up one day and the secret police had removed every screen from their home. How would they feel? Their responses were all along the same lines, and reflect how important the screen has become in their lives.

> 'I would be bored, unexcited and upset. I'd probably commit suicide. It's hard to imagine a world without them. I would not last a minute.' *9 year old boy*

> 'I couldn't live without Game Boy. I'd get too bored.' *8 year old boy*

> 'I would scream the whole house down. I'd be very very sad. Life would be really boring. I wouldn't be able to see my favourite TV show and that would be boring.' *9 year old girl*

It was the prospect of being bored which they dreaded the most. And who can blame them? The screen has become a great source of entertainment – not just for kids, but for adults too.

And one of the things that kids find most appealing about the screen is the variety and flexibility it offers when it comes to entertainment. There's an ever-increasing choice of programmes and games, and you can watch or play them almost anywhere. Many TV and computer games stir up important emotions. Excitement, tension, or just a good laugh.

'Their favourite programme is My Parents are Aliens. It's great to see them having such a belly laugh. They watch it from start to finish. It's just light-hearted entertainment which gets them into hysterics.'
Cheryl, mum with three kids aged 8–15

'Kids are so lucky today. The entertainment's all there for them – on the screen. There's something for everyone – whatever your age, or your likes or dislikes. I find the choice sometimes quite mind boggling.'
Sally Ann, a media enthusiastic mum with two kids

'They love the Disney Channel, things like Lilo & Stitch. They really get into those characters. And films like The Incredibles really get their imagination going. They were jumping about trying to be superheroes.'
Karen, mum with two active boys aged 6 and 8

And let's not forget the benefits for parents too. If the kids are being entertained, then it makes our lives as mums and dads that much less stressful. It gives us time and space to get on and do other things.

Relaxation

We shouldn't underestimate the role the screen plays in allowing our kids just to relax. Parents talk about their kids being under pressure. They recognise the need for them occasionally just to chill out. And there's no doubt that at the end of a school day half an hour in front of the TV, for instance, can restore energy levels so a child's ready to tackle any homework.

'Laura will use the TV to chill out for half an hour.'
Sophie, mum with two girls aged 6 and 9

'I think they have such a high workload that it's entirely right that they veg out in front of the TV from time to time.'
Lucinda, at-home mum with three kids under 12

Louise says:

'I often use the TV simply as a means of giving the kids some down time. It's great for relaxing them, particularly at the end of the afternoon if we've been busy doing something and there's half an hour to fill before tea. There's a limit, after all, to the amount of activity a two and a three year old can take. Occasionally they just need to sit down and flop.'

Education

Whoever you speak to – kids, parents or teachers – everybody agrees that modern media is great for learning. As one teacher said:

> 'As a teacher, I have found a completely new world has opened up in education with the introduction of interactive white boards and the internet. We can link children to live pictures of hurricanes, different animals and a whole range of teaching material through interactive media.'
> Head Teacher

> 'I was teaching about the Second World War and the children being evacuated. I could show the class real clips of this happening. They were so much more involved and it gave them a deeper level of understanding, especially emotionally.' History Teacher

Teachers are also quick to point out that modern media can be a great tool for children with special needs.

If kids have language processing difficulties computer skills can be invaluable. Touch-typing helps kids with poor fine motor control develop hand-eye coordination. It also gives them a sense of pride in their work and confidence that they can produce something legible and literate. Children who need a kinaesthetic approach to learning also benefit particularly from computer learning. And spelling games are excellent for children with poor auditory memory because they encourage them to spend time on learning how to spell.

> 'Computer games certainly have their role. They can be great for getting kids to think around problem solving.' Maths Teacher

> 'A child in my class had poor fine motor skills, which meant that he started to get behind in his work. We noticed a real improvement when he started using the mouse.' Special Needs Teacher

And let's not forget, children learn a lot from the screen by just having fun – whether they're just playing computer games or visiting websites.

'When you're using the computer and the internet you have to read. With a lot of the sites like Polly Pocket and Barbie, you're reading things as you get the next instruction.' *Elena, American mum with kids aged 8–14*

'If you cruise web sites a lot of the information is written. With Mary-Kate and Ashley, for example, you have to do a lot of reading.'
Nikky, mum of one daughter aged 11

'Flight simulators. There's so much to think about in them. I guess they are good for kids because they make them think.'
John, dad of two boys aged 9 and 14

'Playing cricket, it's a calm computer game with things to think about. Like fantasy football, you're constantly planning. All the thinking must be good for them.' *Katie, mum of four kids aged 6–13*

Parents were also keen to quote TV documentaries which had inspired a special interest in their kids.

'People say those history drama documentaries are dumbed down, but I think they are "shoved up" compared to what we were taught at school.'
Sophie, mum of two girls aged 6 and 9

'The TV can give you access to amazing people. These people are the best in their fields and they're there, telling you personally about one thing or another. Kids learn from them.' *Sam, dad with four kids aged 9–14*

'There are great educational programmes on TV. The secret is to be selective. We've built up a library of nature films from the TV which the children love to watch.' *Teacher of 6–10 year olds*

At every stage of learning, the TV and computer are playing a fundamental role in our kids' education.

1. Preschool and early learning

There are lots of examples of quality programmes aimed at the under-fives which encourage different learning opportunities – particularly the development of language skills. For kids of this age it's very easy to mix learning with entertainment, so a lot of the programmes are designed to be fun and educational. Music, songs and rhymes are used to make particular points or teach certain things.

CBeebies is an example of an excellent specialist TV channel and online service aimed at this age group. Many of their programmes are specifically created to help language development and to introduce children to the world around them. If you watch programmes like the Tweenies and Fimbles, for instance, you'll notice educational themes throughout them.

Teresa says:

'Playhouse Disney is a wonderful online resource for this age group. It has a variety of fun activities such as print and play activity sheets and interactive story books. Isabel used to enjoy exploring these online sites with Hugo. It's a good way of getting an older sibling to have a bit of fun with a younger brother or sister.'

Louise says:

'One of Ophelia and Alice's favourite videos is Barney. Barney's a good example of how songs can be used to help develop a child's language and vocabulary. The children have fun dancing round the room singing the songs, and as they're doing it, they're learning new words and expressions.'

19

'My daughter used to watch Countdown when she was 3 and she learnt the alphabet from it. It was incredible. It did help.'
Karen, mum of two girls aged 6 and 8

'Sesame Street is great where they concentrate on one letter at a time, and it really helps extend a child's vocabulary.'
Kim, mum with a boy and a girl aged 5 and 9

2. 5 to 8 year olds

For this age group, the screen is particularly useful for re-inforcing what kids are learning at school. There is a wealth of educational software that appeals to the 5–8 year olds and complements their schoolwork.

Kids of this age are learning the basics – reading, writing and counting. A lot of it can be quite repetitive and boring. Educational TV and computer games inject an element of fun and variety.

'There are some wonderful games for children that support numeracy, learning the alphabet and word building. Visual activities such as matching and pattern making can also be presented in a fun and interactive way on the computer.' *Head Teacher*

'The CBeebies website is fantastic. There's so much good stuff for young kids. There are a lot of different games which you can learn things from. And it's also good because it gets them to follow instructions and improve their mouse control.'
Liz, mum with three kids aged 6–10

'The BBC website is a great source of information for the kids. The other day William was doing a school project and went to it to find out about Celsius and Fahrenheit. He was gripped by all the information he found.'
Kate, city mum with two boys and a girl aged 2–7

Teresa says:

'I have just started using the DK Learning Ladder with Hugo, aged 6. He is a whizz when it comes to computer games, but he has been struggling at school with the basics. Like so many little boys he finds it difficult to focus in class.

I sensed he had fallen behind and realised I needed to do more work with him at home to help him catch up. Sitting at a table with mum doing spellings can be a bit dull, so I thought we would split his homework time – time with me at the table, and time with me at the computer.

So far so good. The DK package is full of fun exercises that get him practising the basics – for example, phonics, spelling, numbers, adding and subtracting. He loves the screen and is proud that he can take control of the computer. The programme gives him lots of positive feedback which spurs him on to focus for a good length of time.'

3. The 8-plus years

The screen for kids of this age group is important because it can empower them to learn independently. As one eight year old girl said, *'It gives us a break from the teachers.'*

The internet and educational CD Roms inspire children to pursue their own agenda. This sense of empowerment and learning things for oneself can be very motivating. If something interests a child, they can go off on their own and find out more. The information world is only a click away.

The computer also enables kids to present their work in new and exciting ways. For kids of this age group, this is particularly appealing. A lot of teachers describe the pride children take in their work when it is typed up and well displayed with a good word processing package. Choosing computer images and different-sized fonts can all add to the fun of doing schoolwork, which in turn can help keep a child interested and motivated.

And, no matter the age of your child, the screen itself can bring any subject to life in the most extraordinary and exciting ways. Children become passionate about history and the importance of strategic planning because of battle games. They get into business planning because of games like RollerCoaster Tycoon, or develop a love for wildlife and geography through nature and travel documentaries.

> 'My 8 year old son plays a computer game called Medieval: Total War. He's learnt a lot more from it than he would ever have done from books. It's taught him how historic battles were fought and how to think strategically.'
> Rachel, a country mum with three kids between 3 and 12

The internet and computer also give learning a sense of topicality, and it's always more fun learning about things that are up to the minute.

> 'My son was doing a project on New Zealand. We were told to look at a particular website at a given time. We sat down and looked at it and all witnessed a geyser erupting. It was happening there before our very eyes – in real time. It just brought the whole thing alive and made the project so much more exciting for him.' Kate, a mum who enjoys learning with her kids

> 'I always found learning French so dull because we used boring old textbooks. Now students can access topical material off the internet in the languages they are learning, and that makes it so much more interesting.'
> Director of online language company

Creative interactive learning experiences can certainly be more effective than the traditional approach. Kids not only enjoy the experience of learning, but learn more too.

Social opportunities

The internet and mobile phones provide all sorts of opportunities for kids to stay in contact with friends and family. They don't even have to leave their home. They can email, text or phone at any time of day to find out what different mates are doing or thinking.

The socialising doesn't just stop with friends. Many children are living a highly social life on the web and forming new friendships. Email has been a great way for kids from different countries to talk to each other. Many schools have set up connections with schools abroad, and communicating via email has made the relationships so much more immediate and rewarding.

Teresa says:

'Isabel, at the age of twelve, uses email and MSN to keep up with her old school mates. Last year we moved and she had to leave a group of girls that she had been with since the age of four. It was pretty tough for her, but knowing there is always a gang of them online after school has been a great comfort to her.'

And TV and computer programmes also provide lots of opportunities for social chitchat. A lot of playground talk revolves around what's been on TV, the storylines in the soaps or the latest computer games. Playing multi-player games, and taking part in online gaming, can bring family and friends together.

'We enjoy Scrapheap Challenge. You never know how it's going to end. We have a bet on which team is going to win. It's more than just a programme, it's us coming together as a family.' *Jennie, mum with three kids aged 2–8*

'Strictly Come Dancing. My daughter's really bubbly after it. She'll talk about it with us all and tell us how she's looking forward to the next one.' *Susan, mum with two daughters aged 6 and 8*

We spoke to one dad who plays a game of FIFA with his seventeen year old son every night. For him it was a special moment – time alone with his son doing an activity they both enjoyed.

'Two-player games can be a great way of getting children together. In no time they just blank out anything in the world around them. If I walk in and say it's tea, they won't hear me. But if Tom says to his friend "did you see that shot?", his friend will reply "great shot". They won't see me, but they are with each other. There's a huge bonding going on.' *Kate, with four kids aged 6–13*

23

Fuels interests

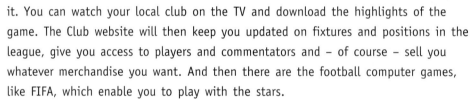

Modern media can motivate children to take up hobbies or follow particular interests. We came across a lot of children who had become interested in something through a TV programme or computer game, and then used the internet to develop the interest.

Football immediately springs to mind. The TV and computer have done wonders to promote a love of the sport. Just think about it. You can watch your local club on the TV and download the highlights of the game. The Club website will then keep you updated on fixtures and positions in the league, give you access to players and commentators and – of course – sell you whatever merchandise you want. And then there are the football computer games, like FIFA, which enable you to play with the stars.

But it's not just popular sports that the screen supports. The internet is great for promoting all sorts of minority interests.

Teresa says:

'My children have been wanting to get a dog for some time. We've been using the internet to help us with the project. To start with we were able to identify what breed we wanted by surfing the web. And then when we had decided to go for a Nova Scotia Retriever, the internet enabled us to get in touch with – and become part of – a whole community around this particular breed.'

Modern media – through the news and internet – also encourages kids to take more of an interest in the world around them.

 'I'd say kids are very politically aware because of the TV. My seven year old has really been following the American elections. He's fascinated by it.'
Fiona, with two boys and a girl aged 7–13

'I think they know more than I do. Programmes like Newsround put it all in a very accessible way. They wouldn't read the newspaper, but they'll watch it on the TV.' *Julia, with two kids aged 10 and 12*

Encourages creativity

There are lots of software packages that inspire the creative child.

Teresa says:

'Isabel, for example, recently came back from school excited about a programme she's been working on in ICT. It's called 'Storyteller' and it allows her to make little films and cartoons. She can use recorded voices and actions, and has a wide choice of people and props.

This is a good example of how the computer can draw out the creative skills of a child. Isabel enjoys creative writing and the programme is like a magical blank sheet of paper. She has to initiate the creative thought, but she has a fabulous set of tools that can really bring her story to life.

Isabel has also had great pleasure from 'Creative Writer', which she started using when she was seven years old. The programme allows her to present any written work – like short stories or poems – professionally with illustrations.'

Likewise, we came across musical children in our research who have been captivated by the composing opportunities offered by computer software. Once again the packages give them a blank sheet of magical paper. It's up to them to think up the composition from scratch, but the tricky bits are made easier for them. So, for example, writing harmonies is made simple. This inspires children to do so much more than they could do just by themselves.

And again, there are packages for the artistic child like *Adobe Photoshop*. This enables the artistically minded child to produce work that could only have been produced by professionals a few years ago. Kids can, for example, scan in visuals and create professional style montages and graphic designs.

But even standard *Word* can be used in a creative way.

Teresa says:

'Isabel, again, has been inspired by the ability to produce work in a book format. She has written a couple of little books inspired by this simple bit of software. For her it is much more fun when the final product looks really professional.

Isabel also uses a simple package called *Paint*. This allows her to create her own visuals that can then be copy pasted into her *Word* document. Recently she even made a story page for her younger brother Hugo who is having difficulty learning to spell. She popped the words Hugo was trying to learn into an illustrated story book – leaving gaps for Hugo to fill in. Hugo was chuffed to be given a worksheet by his sister with computer illustrations, and Isabel had fun on the computer producing it.'

Kids and parents talked about their favourite websites and TV programmes that encouraged them to be creative:.

'Art Attack is so inspiring. It teaches you how to draw a horse by showing the skeleton first. Then they draw a fairy and make it look magical by simply rubbing the chalk dust out to one side. My daughter was up and out of the room. She wanted to have a go.' *Liz, mum with three kids aged 6–10*

'Children love the cookery programmes. They really get them wanting to have a go.' *Barb, mum with two kids aged 3 and 6*

'Blue Peter still does it for my kids. The sticky glue, the fluffy animals, the presenters – everything about it gets them interested and excited.' *Emma, mum with three kids aged 5–10*

'Lego racers is really exciting. It gets him doing things. He'll jump and build an island or a racing track – or just use his imagination to do whatever takes his fancy.' *Hilary, mum with three kids aged 7–13*

'We love the Playhouse Disney site. We've done loads of projects from it.' *Debs, mum with one daughter aged 7*

'I'm quite techy myself so there's plenty of opportunity for our kids to try things out on the screen. Even our two year old son is having fun painting and drawing on the computer. And the great thing about it, there's no mess to clear up after.' *Charlie, IT consultant dad*

There are also lots of websites that invite children to send in their creative work. Knowing that your work is going to be pasted up in a public place can be a great incentive for producing something creative.

IT literacy

Mouse control. Eye and hand coordination. Surfing. Emailing. It's important that kids get familiar with technology before they enter the adult world. The more competent they are with the screen, the easier they'll find the transition into a working environment.

'At IBM we live completely off our laptops. We receive everything electronically. I no longer have an in-tray for letters — we just don't work with paper. Obviously if our new recruits have plenty of experience with computers that's a significant advantage.' *Andrew, IBM consultant*

'It's the way of the world. The screen is the medium of communication, information and education. Learning to use a computer is as important as learning to hold a pen.' *Neil, dad with kids aged 6–12, garage sales representative*

Independence

Kids, in particular, highlighted how modern media is giving them more freedom and independence.

The most obvious example is mobile phones. These give parents the courage to allow children a bit more freedom because they know they can always stay in touch. And, as we've seen, the screen enables kids to do all sorts of things – learn, socialise, have fun, discover the world – without the help of an adult.

And then there's electronic voting and interactive participation. Kids have found a new voice. They don't have to wait until they are 18, and can vote in a general election to be heard. In an interactive media age their views and opinions matter. They can vote for their favourite pop star or celebrity act, give instant feedback on what they've seen on TV by emailing programmes, or even set up their own website to express their views and opinions to the world.

 It's exciting to see people using their brains alongside the telly in the new interactive quiz shows like Test The Nation. Online quizzes and online voting introduce a new form of democracy, which is welcome.'
Interactive TV consultant

Chapter 2

Media dangers — what every parent should know about media bingeing

SO IS IT THAT DAMAGING?

'I do think, should I shout 'turn that computer off' and get her to come and sit with me? But then is it that damaging when she's on there having her own fun? Why should I bring her in here? Do I want her in here for me? I don't know. I don't know!'

Paula, single mum with 12 year old daughter

→ **A question that vexed this mum ... should she, or shouldn't she try and get things into balance?**

So, if kids are having fun — and often learning things too — what's the worry? The concern is that if children are spending too much time in front of the TV and computer — particularly over 2 hours a day — they can be harmed in all sorts of ways.

We have outlined five areas for parents to keep an eye on:

- Behaviour
- Physical well-being
- Education
- Relationships
- World outlook

In each area we look at specific problems arising from too much screen consumption, describing the symptoms and examining the different influences of the media. In many cases there will obviously be other contributing factors to a child's specific condition, but for the purpose of The Media Diet we are looking solely at the impact of too much media on our kids.

We're not scientists ourselves and don't pretend to be. A lot of what follows is what we have gathered from our own research, from talking to people with first-hand experience of kids – and from the kids themselves. We've also been monitoring studies published in recent years and have included some of the facts which impressed us the most.

Think of this section as a checklist. See if you recognise any of the symptoms in your child. Hopefully you won't, and hopefully it won't all sound too scary. It's not meant to be. But we thought it was important for you to know exactly what you're up against before you get started on The Media Diet.

YES, TOO MUCH IS DAMAGING

... and there's plenty of evidence to prove it

1. BEHAVIOUR

1. BEHAVIOUR

- Anti-social behaviour
- Impulsive outbursts
- Play apathy
- Depression
- Premature adulthood

By the age of 18 the average child in the US has witnessed 200,000 acts of violence on the TV.[2] And that's even before you add up all the hours of shooting and fighting on their PlayStations and computers.

You don't need to be a scientist to work out that kids mimic what they see. Of course they do. Any parent knows that. If children watch things on the screen, they'll often want to copy them. It's natural.

The advertising world knows only too well about the 'mimicking power' of the screen. In fact they positively exploit it.

Teresa says

'I particularly remember the "You've been Tangoed" campaign. It was a wow of a campaign for the soft drinks company and the slap across the face always prompted a laugh. The only problem was the effect it was having on kids. Schools started reporting playground tears as the slapping game became a national craze.'

NO QUESTION ABOUT MIMICKING

'I know that he mimics what he sees on TV ... you should have seen him the other day ... there he was cutting his hair ... apparently some kid did it on his favourite show! But does that mean he will be affected by the violence he sees?'

Charlotte, mum of two kids aged 4 and 6

Even film people agree that too much violence on the TV isn't a good thing – 80 per cent of Hollywood executives believe there is a link between TV violence and the real thing.[3] And now, parents are actually suing a media company because of the harmful influence of a violent computer game.

In the first case of its kind, Mr and Mrs Pakeerah of Leicester are suing a media company for the death of their son, Stefan. They claim the friend who killed their son was inspired by one of the scenes in the game Manhunt.

In Germany many people believe that the Gutenburg school killer – who went on a shooting rampage in his old school – was also motivated by video games. The head of the school's parents' committee, and father of one of the surviving children, said:

'People go into an artificial world, they go into something like a trance. We know he played video games ... the way he fulfilled this killing was very similar to the games he played. The black dressing he had was completely like the killer in the game.'

As a result, laws in Germany were changed to restrict the sale of violent games. These include products where violence is the sole purpose of the game, and those where violence is portrayed in a cynical, comical or glamorised way.

Aggressive Scripts

Professor Barbara Krahe at The University of Potsdam believes that in both the Pakeerah and Gutenburg cases the killer may have been playing out an 'aggressive script'. As she says:

'Once the threshold to be violent has passed, then the person just follows a pattern. The game could have provided such a script. You don't have to decide for every action, what am I going to do next. You just follow the script.'[4]

The concept of 'violent thresholds' has been discussed by Centrewall and Lt. Col Dave Grossman, a military psychologist who has helped train soldiers to kill. According to Grossman, the evidence for linking the media with the rising levels of violence in society is stronger than the link between lung cancer and smoking.

He argues that the electronic media has shifted our 'violence threshold' because video games include many of the techniques that the military use to shift 'violence thresholds' and encourage soldiers to kill. As a result, people more prone to violence are more likely to become violent.[5]

TRAINING SOLDIERS TO KILL

- Conditioning and rewarding
- Repetition
- Training knee-jerk reactions
- Role-modelling
- Desensitisation

 Techniques that remove a soldier's inhibitions ...

 Techniques that are evident in the most violent games

... AND IF YOU STILL NEED CONVINCING

... read the following facts and figures to stir you into action

34

Behaviour – facts and figures

Anti-social behaviour

Symptoms: No respect for others – mimicking screen bad behaviour.

 Media Alert: Screen behaviour becomes the norm. Bad role models. Violence glamorised.

FACT 1:

Parents and teachers have plenty of first-hand experience of children mimicking bad behaviour from the TV or computer games.[6]

'Anti-social behaviour is a problem because they do mimic – for example, the words from programmes like Tracy Beaker or The Simpsons.'
Sharon, mum who's aware of TV mimicking

'I find after they've been watching Power Rangers their behaviour becomes violent – particularly towards my husband and me.'
City mum worried about the effect of some TV on her sons

'Mum got an 18 once, but my younger brother started acting all violent, and his friends started acting violent too. It was Grand Theft Auto: Vice City. There is a lady with G-strings and they are going for her with the chainsaw. They got all mental. And they started doing it at school. My mum stopped me from playing it, even though it was my younger brother who was acting violent.'   *12 year old boy*

'I was arguing with my brother and I put it in his neck. Like I'd seen in sumo wrestling. Putting the elbow in the back of the neck, it's really dangerous.'
11 year old boy

'Some programmes do cause aggression in children, we see it in the classroom. I've seen children clenching their fists when talking about a particularly violent programme. Terminator was one. I'd then see them rushing into the playground hitting each other.'
Su, Head Teacher

FACT 2:

A major review of recent research concluded there is consistent evidence that violent imagery has substantial short-term effects on the arousal, thoughts and emotions of children, increasing the likelihood of aggressive and fearful behaviour in younger children, particularly boys. The study was conducted by Kevin Browne and Catherine Hamilton-Giachritsis at Birmingham University.[7]

FACT 3:

Research has shown that children who watch excessive amounts of TV are more likely to become bullies. A study by Dr Frederick Zimmerman of The University of Washington, Seattle, found that children aged six to eleven who were categorised as bullies watched on average 5 hours of TV a day, compared to 3.2 hours watched by non-bullies.[8]

This supports work by Sarah Coyne of The University of Central Lancashire. She found that girls who had watched the most indirect aggression, such as bullying, on TV were perceived as being more aggressive by their peers.

Sarah Coyne suggested that if young people overdose on programmes that are full of characters bad mouthing each other, back biting and rumour spreading, this may encourage them to use this form of aggression in their own behaviour.[9]

FACT 4:

Switching off the TV can reduce aggression in children, according to a study led by Thomas Robinson of Stanford University School of Medicine. He observed how a group of 8 to 9 year olds whose TV and video viewing was cut by over a half to seven hours a week, showed a reduction in violent behaviour by 25 per cent.[10]

Impulsive outbursts

Symptoms: Low level of tolerance/easily frustrated – leading to bad temper. Physical and verbal outbursts. Constant swearing becomes the norm. Not prepared to wait for anything.

 Media Alert: Sedentary existence/bottled-up energy. Instant gratification of TV and compulsive character of computer games. Inability to express self through language. Swearing on screen.

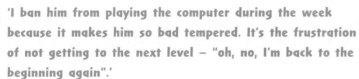

FACT 1:

Parents describe how hours spent in front of the screen can leave a child prone to explosive bursts of energy and bad temper.[6]

  'I ban him from playing the computer during the week because it makes him so bad tempered. It's the frustration of not getting to the next level – "oh, no, I'm back to the beginning again".'
Jackie, mum of a 12 year old boy – a tight controller

  'I find TV makes them bad tempered in the mornings. I find they're much nicer if they haven't watched it.'
Lucinda, mum of three under 10 – trying to take to control

  'Computer games make them so irritable and competitive. I've definitely noticed that with my daughter. She gets very stroppy if she can't get to that end point. She's shouting at the computer.'
Sally, a mum aware of how computer games affect moods

FACT 2:

There is a general feeling that children are more impulsive than before, and that this may well be related to the character of screen media – for example, the immediacy of the TV experience and impulsive character of many computer games.

Grandmothers, in particular, speak of children being less patient than they used to be.[6]

'They want to be there and be noticed all the time. They have no patience and expect you to pay attention immediately.'
Julia, grandmother in country village

'The telly and computer make everything seem too immediate. It's hard for kids to realise that sometimes you have to wait for things.'
Dawn, city grandmother

FACT 3:

Parents are concerned about the increase in bad language amongst children, and many of them blame the new generation of TV and computer games. Interestingly fathers seem more concerned about the swearing their sons pick up from the games than the violence they are watching.[6]

'Everybody is swearing – even the 10-year-olds at the football club. I wasn't swearing at 10 – I knew it was wrong. It is now part of everyday language.'
Neil, dad with 2 sons and a daughter. Football coach in spare time

'Computer games use it as part of the game – 10 years ago, they wouldn't have got away with it.'
Chris, dad of an 8 and 10 year old. Salesman

'Presenters talking about how pissed they got the night before, and how bad their hangovers are.'
Nicky, mum of a 7 and 9 year old. Concerned about media values

Play apathy

Symptoms: Difficulty playing away from the screen. Always turning to adults to be entertained. Easily bored.

 Media Alert: Too much time in front of the TV and computer can hinder a child's ability to play imaginatively.

FACT 1:

Kids say that too much screen time makes them feel apathetic.[6]

'If I've been in front of the screen too long I feel lazy and unhealthy. Really clogged up.' *12 year old girl*

'It's when I get off I get bored. You think what am I going to do now?'
12 year old girl

FACT 2:

Many carers and parents have experienced the problem of play apathy. They describe how kids can't play with traditional toys or simply create their own fantasy games. They note that play apathy is at its worst after a child has spent long periods of time in front of the screen.[6]

'My son has some friends who play on their PlayStation all the time and I've noticed that those children have difficulty playing imaginatively. They come to the house and all they want to do is use the Game Boy.'
Lucinda – at-home city mum

'If I have had a busy work week and I've let my five-year-old spend too long in front of the TV, I find he becomes worse at playing with his other toys. It's as though he forgets how to play with them.' *Jo – working city mum*

'The only thing that seems to keep John's attention is the TV. If I get out a selection of toys from the cupboard for him to play with, he'll go from one to another, never spending more than five minutes with any particular one.'
Christine, part-time working mum, having difficulty occupying son

Depression

Symptoms: Sense of depression and low self esteem.

 Media Alert: Long periods in front of the screen leading to frustration.

FACT 1:

The rate of emotional problems such as anxiety and depression has increased by 70 per cent since the mid-1980s amongst adolescents, according to a study by the Institute of Psychiatry, King's College London and the University of Manchester.[11]

FACT 2:

Children are quick to admit that too much screen time can leave them feeling depressed and frustrated. It puts them in a bad mood and they sense that all too often they take it out on their parents.[6]

> 'I think TV makes you feel depressed. Like all you're doing is watching people better than you, or worse than you.' *11 year old girl*

> 'Just sitting in a dark room watching TV makes you feel depressed, makes you moody. It doesn't make you happy like you've achieved something.' *12 year old girl*

> 'I get bored and annoyed with myself because I haven't got anything else done.' *11 year old girl*

> 'I feel frustrated after computer games. There's always something you haven't completed.' *9 year old boy*

> 'I'm really loony if I've been on the computer too long. Hard to deal with for my parents. Shouting a lot. Can't be bothered mood.' *11 year old girl*

Premature adulthood

Symptoms: Acting older than your age without maturity of that age. Superficially in the know about sex, but deep down confused about it all. Getting involved in under-age sex. Visiting sex and porn sites.

 Media Alert: Over-exposure to adult viewing and material. Introduced to explicit character of sex before understanding role of different relationships. Easy to surf into dirty territory.

FACT 1:

Children are more exposed to pornography as a result of the internet.

Nearly 60 per cent of 9 to 19 year olds who go online at least once a week have experienced online pornography, and 36 per cent have *accidentally* found themselves on a pornographic website. One third of them have received unwanted sexual or nasty comments.[12]

Children are also more exposed to adult TV viewing. On average, kids aged 4 to 15 years watch more TV in adult airtime than in children's airtime – 12 hours, as opposed to 5 hours a week.[13]

FACT 2:

Parents are concerned about their kids being over-exposed to sex at an early age, and many of them have experienced the problems of easy-to-find sex and porn sites on the internet. Parents are worried that children think they are in the know about sex and relationships, but haven't the maturity to understand how it all fits into real life.[6]

'One thing that has concerned me is all the premarital sex. I read a statistic that Rachel on Friends had had 829 one-night stands.'
Elena, mum of two girls and a boy

'MTV is the worst. The gang warfare. It's the attitude. Very sexually explicit street talk.' *Sharon, mum of 2 boys. Worried about violence on her estate*

FACT 3:

An excess of TV can also have a physiological effect on how a child matures, according to research by Professor Roberto Salti of the Meyer's Children Hospital at the University of Florence.

Professor Salti claims that the light and radiation emitted from TV and computer screens disturb the production of the hormone melatonin. He goes on to conclude that this may be one of the factors that speed up the onset of puberty.[14]

2. Physical well-being

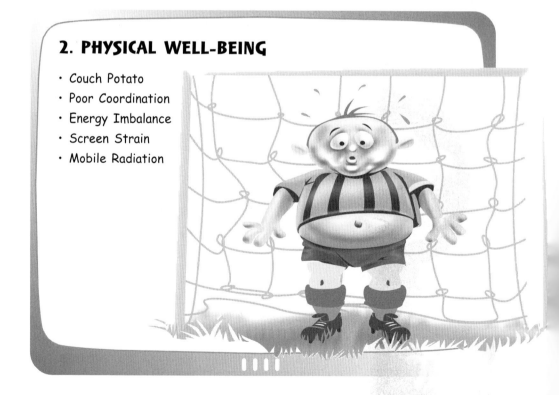

2. PHYSICAL WELL-BEING

- Couch Potato
- Poor Coordination
- Energy Imbalance
- Screen Strain
- Mobile Radiation

'Don't sit in front of the TV, or you'll get square eyes!'

Do you remember being told that as a child? We do. And it didn't half annoy us at the time. But our mums had a point. And today, it isn't just square eyes that we should be warning our kids against. The biggest health hazard of sitting for hours in front of a screen is simply that you're inactive. Kids need active bodies to have healthy bodies.

The World Health Organization has reported that physical inactivity is one of the ten leading causes of death in developed countries, producing around 2 million deaths worldwide per year.[15]

There is a clear trend towards children leading a less active lifestyle. As Sandy Livingstone of Enlightenment Consultants comments:

'Children have always eaten things which aren't necessarily good for them, but the new problem is that increasingly they're not burning off the calories. They're spending less time exercising and more time in front of the screen. This must be a major factor contributing to the problem of rising child obesity.'

... AND IF YOU STILL NEED CONVINCING

... read the following facts and figures to stir you into action

Physical well-being – facts and figures

Couch potato

Symptoms: Being so overweight that a child's health is at risk from, for example, heart disease, diabetes, some cancers and musculo-skeletal problems. Physically unfit.

 Media Alert: Too much time just sitting – and snacking – in front of the screen.

FACT 1:

Obesity in the UK – like in many other countries – is on the rise. The number of obese individuals increased threefold between 1980 and 2002. In 2002, 30 per cent of children were at least overweight and 16 per cent were obese. In less than ten years, obesity has doubled amongst boys and increased by 60 per cent amongst girls.

It's estimated that if current rates continue, a third of all adults will be obese by 2010, bringing levels of obesity up to those currently experienced in the USA.[16]

FACT 2:

Children and teenagers who watch more than two hours of TV a day are more at risk of being overweight and having poor cardiovascular fitness by the time they reach the age of 26. This was the finding of researchers from the University of Otago, New Zealand, who followed 1,000 children born in 1972 and 1973 from the age of three up to the age of 26.

More specifically, the researchers claimed that 17 per cent of weight problems, 15 per cent of raised blood cholesterol and 15 per cent of poor cardiovascular fitness in 26-year-olds, could be linked to excessive TV viewing in childhood and adolescence.

Dr Robert Hancox, who led the study, said:

'Our results suggest that excessive television viewing in young people is likely to have far-reaching consequences for adult health.'[17]

FACT 3:

One in five teenagers is suffering from early signs of heart disease and stroke, according to research by Dr Faisel Khan of Dundee University. The research found that poor diet and an inactive lifestyle is having an impact on children's health.[18]

FACT 4:

Type 2 diabetes – which is associated with obesity – can be directly linked with TV viewing. In the US research has shown that men who consistently watch more than 21 hours of TV a week double their risk of getting this form of diabetes.[19]

Poor coordination

Symptoms: Clumsiness and lack of bodily coordination. This isn't just a physical problem but can lead to early learning problems, for example, recognising shapes and writing skills.

 Media Alert: Being entertained in a sedentary way, rather than being active doing physical play. Too many armchair sportsmen.

FACT 1:

Child experts are noticing that children are becoming more prone to poor co-ordination.

 'Children are not encouraged to spend as much time crawling or exploring their physical environments as they once were. We have children who are not growing up with adequate coordination.'
Phyllis Weikart, a child development expert[20]

Energy imbalance

Symptoms: Either a surplus of energy (hyperactivity), or a lack of energy (inertia).

 Media Alert: Long periods of time in front of the screen without physical activity.

FACT 1:

Parents say that sitting in front of a screen for a long period affects a child's energy levels. Parents describe how a two-hour stint on a racing game can leave a child full of nervous energy, while two hours flopping in front of the TV can leave a child too lethargic to do anything.[6]

'My child seems to go through continual highs and lows. One minute he's racing round the house pretending he's an aeroplane or a soldier on the attack – the next moment I can't even drag him off the sofa to come and have some supper. It's impossible to judge him. Either it seems as if he's high on something, or else it's as though all the energy has been sucked out of him.'

Karen, at-home city mum, with two energetic boys

'I think it makes them quite hyper and aggravated – especially if they haven't won.'

Susan, part-time working mum, with computer-obsessed boys.

Screen strain

Symptoms: Repetitive Strain Injury (RSI), musculo-skeletal injuries, computer elbow, back, neck and eye ache.

 Media Alert: Constant repetitive movements and poor posture as a result of hours sitting in front of the screen. Kids are particularly vulnerable because their bones and muscles are still developing.

FACT 1:

Hours spent in front of the TV or computer screen, combined with carrying heavy school bags, are blamed for a 5 per cent increase in children with backache, according to The British Chiropractic Association (BCA). A survey by the BCA found that the sedentary lifestyle of many kids is putting them at risk of developing back pain later in life.[21]

FACT 2:

Anyone who spends more than two hours a day working on a computer may be at risk of developing eye strain and focusing difficulties, according to the American Optometric Association. The Association reported that computers can exacerbate conditions like nearsightedness or myopia.

Dr Cary Herzberg, an optometrist in Aurora, Illinois said:

'As children spend more time on the computer and at other near-point tasks, their risk of developing myopia increases. We are definitely seeing more children now with this type of problem than we did five years ago.'[22]

FACT 3:

Parents and children are all too aware of the strain and pain the screen can cause.[6]

'It's bad for you. It's bad for your eyes.'
10 year old boy

'After about one or two hours on the computer I go dizzy.'
8 year old girl

'I feel it after a couple of hours. Your eyes go all achey.'
9 year old boy

'My 5 year old developed blisters on his thumbs because he was playing so much – I was worried what his teachers would think – it was probably obvious what it was from.' *Fiona, part-time working mum*

Mobile radiation

Symptoms: Not yet fully known or proved. If there is a danger, children may be more at risk because their skulls are thinner than adults.

 Media Alert: Young children's use of mobile phones.

FACT 1:

Children under nine years old should not own mobile phones according to Sir William Stewart, Chairman of The Health Protection Agency. He said that scientists were unable to say whether mobiles were safe and advised people to take precautionary action:

'My advice is that they should not have them because children's skulls are not fully thickened, their nervous systems are not fully developed and the radiation penetrates further into their brains.'[23]

3. Education

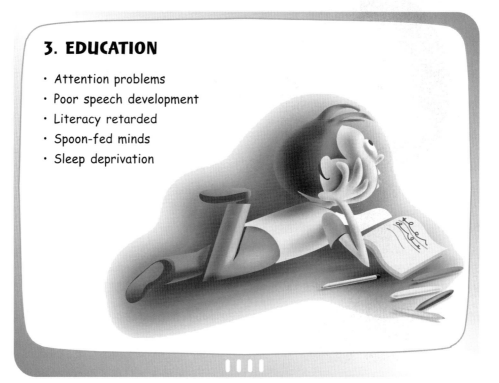

3. EDUCATION

- Attention problems
- Poor speech development
- Literacy retarded
- Spoon-fed minds
- Sleep deprivation

More and more research is proving that too much screen time can be bad for education. It can put pressure on your child's schedule and affect the way they develop intellectually.

In the US, for instance, a study found that over ten hours a week of TV viewing has a negative influence on a child's academic performance, while other research shows that students who watched over six hours a day achieved the lowest academic results.[24]

If you ask any teacher how children have changed over the last few years, one of the things they often mention is that children have shorter attention spans than before. It's not surprising. Kids have got used to screen communication that bombards them with constant visual and audio stimulation. It is a world full of sound-bites that can be absorbed effortlessly by kids.

... AND IF YOU STILL NEED CONVINCING

... read the following facts and figures to stir you into action

Education – facts and figures

Attention problems

Symptoms: Difficulty in focusing on specific tasks ('attention-deficit/hyperactivity disorder'). Child's mind darts around, unable to develop logical trains of thought.

 Media Alert: Child's senses are bombarded by a constant stream of stimuli from the screen. Soundbite character of screen entertainment.

FACT 1:

Hours of television viewing between the ages of one and three are associated with attention problems at the age of seven years old, according to research led by Dimitri Christakis of the Child Health Institute at the University of Washington. Dimitri Christakis monitored over 1,000 children when they were 1, 3 and 7 years old and believes that attention problems arise when a child is exposed to TV while the pathways of their brain are still developing. As a result he recommends that efforts should be made to limit television viewing in early childhood.[25]

FACT 2:

Parents and teachers describe how the TV and computer games encourage short attention spans in children and distract their thought process. They talk about children having butterfly minds that dart from one thing to the next. Thoughts are scrambled together, rather than being logically thought through.[6]

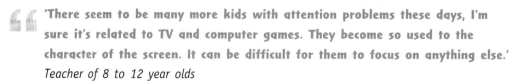
'There seem to be many more kids with attention problems these days, I'm sure it's related to TV and computer games. They become so used to the character of the screen. It can be difficult for them to focus on anything else.' *Teacher of 8 to 12 year olds*

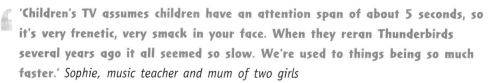
'Children's TV assumes children have an attention span of about 5 seconds, so it's very frenetic, very smack in your face. When they reran Thunderbirds several years ago it all seemed so slow. We're used to things being so much faster.' *Sophie, music teacher and mum of two girls*

'It can be so hard to get them to think things through. Their minds are used to taking in a constant stream of entertainment – it can be hard to get them to think slowly but surely. It can all seem too boring compared to the screen.'
Teacher of 8 to 12 year olds

FACT 3:

The regular use of text messages and emails can knock up to ten points off your IQ. This was the finding from a study completed at the University of London by Dr Glenn Wilson. The research team concluded that the brain finds it hard to cope with juggling lots of tasks at once, reducing its overall effectiveness.

The study described the risks of 'infomania' where individuals are constantly distracted by 'always on' technology. It means that they lose concentration as their minds are in a permanent state of readiness to react to technology, instead of focusing on the task in hand.[26]

FACT 4:

The TV is preventing children concentrating properly on their homework. Research shows that most children keep the TV on while doing their homework,[27] and that the obsessive character of computer games is also distracting them.[6]

 'If you're stuck on a level, I keep thinking of how I can do the level while I'm doing my homework'. *11 year old boy*

Poor speech development

Symptoms: Slow to develop language and ability to communicate.

 Media Alert: Not enough interaction/conversation with real people. Constant background noise of TV.

FACT 1:

A variety of studies have demonstrated that children who are heavy TV viewers are likely to be linguistically underdeveloped. This is the conclusion of Dr Robin Close, who has reviewed research published over the last 30 years.[28]

She concludes that children who watch large amounts of adult and general programmes – in other words, programmes not specifically targeted at them – are most affected. She points to one study published in 2004 that monitored 6,961 children over time. In this study children under the age of three who did not watch television at all achieved the highest language scores.[29]

On a positive note, she reviews a number of studies that show that a limited amount of educational TV can benefit children, particularly if they have a chance to chatter about the programme. For instance, there are several studies that show that limited viewing of Sesame Street can have a positive influence on language skills.

FACT 2:

An increasing number of children are starting school with under-developed speaking and listening skills, according to a survey of head teachers of primary and nursery schools in Wales. The consensus amongst teachers interviewed was that 'many young children have difficulties in communicating; have little experience of books and stories and know few rhymes or songs'.

Most (nearly two thirds) felt that children's talking and listening skills had declined over the last five years, particularly the ability to speak audibly and to be understood.

Alan Wells, Director of The Basic Skills Agency, gave two reasons for the decline in good communication skills – a shortage of time amongst parents, and 'the readily available attractions that compete with talking and listening'.[30]

FACT 3:

There is concern amongst parents that we are bringing up a generation of grunters.[6]

 **'They're all like, "grunt, grunt". Just grunters. They'll bring up their children to be grunters too. The majority are like that.'** *Keeya, single mum on city estate*

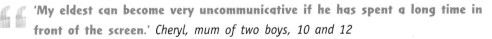 **'My eldest can become very uncommunicative if he has spent a long time in front of the screen.'** *Cheryl, mum of two boys, 10 and 12*

FACT 4:

Listening and attention problems, which can delay language development, have been linked with TV viewing by Dr Sally Ward, a speech and language therapist.

She researched 1,000 pre-school children in Manchester and found that one in five had listening and attention problems that delayed their language development. This figure doubled between 1984 and 1990, coinciding with the extension of breakfast and daytime TV.

She concluded: 'Children are focusing exclusively on the noise from the TV and stereos, and ignoring the human voice. Consequently learning to speak is delayed and other social and educational problems arise.'[31]

Literacy retarded

Symptoms: Slow in developing reading/writing skills.

 Media Alert: Too much media time and no time for reading. Media overshadows fun of learning through books.

FACT 1:

Encouraging children to enjoy reading boosts their literacy. Students who read for pleasure every day scored almost 10 per cent higher on proficiency tests than those who never read for fun.[32]

FACT 2:

Educationalists believe that the sense of balance and movement are important for literacy development, and that if a child's movements are limited by too much TV and computer time their literacy skills can be affected.

For example, some dyslexic children suffer from a kind of motion sickness, where letters move up and down their visual field, or they may be affected by a sense of dizziness as they try to focus on the words. This explains why some dyslexic children have been cured by sea sickness pills.

Dr Harold Levinson explains:

'Researchers discovered that astronauts in space suffer a temporary form of dyslexia, such as reading words upside down and backwards. I began to use the same motion sickness pills that astronauts were given to treat the problems dyslexics have with movement concentration levels, balance and short term memory.'[33]

FACT 3:

Too sedentary a lifestyle can lead to poor coordination, which can result in poor spatial awareness. This means children have difficulty perceiving shapes and this can cause problems with basic reading and writing skills.[6]

 'If kids don't exercise enough they become vulnerable to poor coordination and motor skills. Their spatial awareness is poor and therefore writing and remembering shapes can also become difficult.' *Special Needs Teacher*

Spoon-fed minds

Symptoms: See everything through screen images. Not tapping into your own creative and imaginative resources. Avoiding tasks that challenge your own intellectual thought.

 Media Alert: Media that constantly forces images on viewers can result in the loss of a child's internal space. So much comes on a plate – for example, being able to copy and paste from the internet.

FACT 1:

Parents, teachers and child experts are conscious of how the TV affects children's ability to think. They talk about the unchallenging nature of a lot of screen entertainment.

 'Teachers find that today's video-immersed children can't form original pictures in their minds or develop imaginative representations. It's dreadful because they can't think for themselves. It doesn't teach you to think. There's such an overload of information.' *Jane Healy, an educational psychologist*[34]

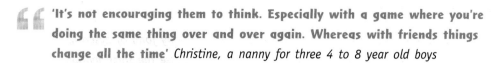 'It's not encouraging them to think. Especially with a game where you're doing the same thing over and over again. Whereas with friends things change all the time' *Christine, a nanny for three 4 to 8 year old boys*

FACT 2:

The wide availability of information and views on the internet can encourage a copy-cat culture. Amongst 12 to 19 year olds who go online regularly, 21 per cent admit to having copied something from the internet for a school project and handing it in as their own.[12]

Sleep deprivation

Symptoms: Too tired to concentrate on anything/nodding off in class.

 Media Alert: Temptation to watch TV/play computer games/text on the mobile after bedtime. Over-stimulation just before trying to get to sleep. TV in bedrooms.

FACT 1:

Kids – when they're away from their parents – are quick to admit they're not getting enough sleep.[6]

 'When my friend had a TV in her room she said it really affected her. She couldn't sleep at night.' *11 year old girl*

 'My two best friends both had TV and laptops, and it really affects their sleeping. At school they say I'm really tired. One of them owned up to her parents that it really affected her, and now she's had it taken out.' *12 year old girl*

FACT 2:

Teachers say that kids often come to school too tired to concentrate properly, and it's often as a result of being up too late in front of the screen.

'Working parents are often too tired to talk to their children in the evening, check their homework is done, or even get them to bed. In some high income homes, televisions and game consoles are being used as "free" babysitters, and children, left to their own devices, are glued to computers.'
David Hart, General Secretary of The National Association of Head Teachers[35]

'There were these 6-year-old twins at school who kept on coming in very tired and would keep on yawning throughout the class. I asked the nanny what was happening and she said the parents – who both worked – insisted that she kept them up until 8.30pm every night so they could see them. They would be plonked in front of videos because they were obviously too tired to do anything else at that time.' *Serena, teacher of 5 to 11 year olds[6]*

FACT 3:

Youngsters playing games, watching TV and texting on mobile phones late into the night are losing up to a month's worth of sleep a year. This was the result of a study by The University of Oxford.

It also found that this lack of sleep was threatening the physical and mental health of up to one million primary-age children.[36]

FACT 4:

Watching three hours or more TV each day leaves teenagers twice as likely to develop sleep problems when they get older, according to a study by Columbia University in New York.

The study, which monitored teenagers and young adults when they were 14, 16 and 22 years old, found that late night television may leave viewers in a state of 'heightened alertness and physiological arousal', preventing then from falling asleep with ease.

It also concluded that being exposed to many hours of the bright light of the television screen may throw them off their sleep-wake pattern. Both factors may become ingrained and cause persistent problems in later years.[37]

4. Relationships

4. RELATIONSHIPS

- Modern-day hermits
- Parents in the dark
- Social overload
- Internet grooming

Developing happy and stable relationships is an important part of growing up. In many ways modern media can be a great 'socialising' force. But it can also cause problems when it comes to relationships.

We asked one single mum to imagine life without the TV or computer. Her first thought was, 'Hooray'. She would regain her relationship with her 12 year old daughter:

'We would talk more. We would do more little things together. We would walk down to the shops together. Do all those things we used to do – before I got her the computer.'

Close relationships deteriorating, or being lost altogether, was the biggest concern for parents with kids who binge on TV and computer games. These children appear to value the screen above anything else and are at risk of becoming loners – or modern-day hermits. We found that it was this loss of social interaction that often prompted parents to take action and cut back on their kids' media consumption.

... AND IF YOU STILL NEED CONVINCING

... read the following facts and figures to stir you into action

Relationships – facts and figures

Modern-day hermits

Symptoms: Going around in your own little world – not interacting with family and friends. Selfish approach to life.

 Media Alert: Satellite living. Bedroom culture where kids' bedrooms become a self-sufficient media centre. Few family meals together.

FACT 1:

80 per cent of 11 to 15 year olds have a TV in their bedroom,[1] and one fifth of 9 to 19 year olds have internet access in their bedrooms.[12]

'The risk is that we become a disconnected society. Quality of life depends on us relating to each other and if we have no opportunity to do that and practise it as we grow up, we may settle for solitary lives, depending on television for entertainment and the internet to communicate.'
Professor Alan Smithers, The University of Buckingham[38]

'Technology is part of our society and a lot of it is extremely educational for children. But there is a danger that they are spending less time in social situations and they miss out on socialising skills. They become isolated from their family as well as their peers.'
Rosemary Duff, Research Director, Childwise[39]

FACT 2:

Sixty per cent of 11 to 14 year olds say that at home everyone is free to get on with their own lives and interests, according to Mintel, the consumer research company. Only 36 per cent of adults actively limit how much TV their children watch, and 53 per cent of children say that as long as they study and do well at school they can do what they like.[40]

Jenny Catlin from Mintel concludes:

'Sadly, it does seem that in many cases modern technology has now replaced the family unit, so that everyone does whatever they want, when they want, even if it means doing it on their own.'

FACT 3:

Some parents have watched their children turn from socially active individuals to moody loners or modern-day hermits, as a result of computer games.[6]

'I've got a 15 year old son. He got really obsessed by it. If you called him for meals he wouldn't hear you. It was only when friends started calling him for football – when he didn't want to play or do things after school – that I said you can only go on it for a certain length of time. I encouraged him to go out more. I think he could have become really quite isolated. I'm conscious of it now.' *Ray, dad with three kids*

 'My friend's girl is hooked on Sims. She doesn't come out of her bedroom.' *Pam, mum with 11 year old daughter*

FACT 4:

Some parents have given up trying to get their kids to do what they want. The kids are leading their lives – and the parents theirs.[6]

 'She comes home at 3.30, puts the computer straight on. She often has her dinner in front of it. It's hard to get her off for dinner. After dinner she'll be back on her computer until bedtime, at 9. I suppose she's on there for at least 5 or 6 hours on a school day. I think at the moment it's too much. Even though Sims isn't bad.' *Uri, mum of 12 year old girl*

 'Another thing is that they don't sit down and talk to each other at the table, they don't sit down and have a meal, it's all on their laps in front of the TV.' *Anne, granny with 8 grandchildren*

Parents in the dark

Symptoms: Parents not in touch with their children's lives. Poor communications/inability to spot when things go wrong.

 Media Alert: Technology whizz kids – out-of-touch parents. Parents lacking language and know-how of modern media.

FACT 1:

Parents are out of touch with what their children are doing on the internet.

Nearly half of 9 to 19 year olds who go online at least once a week have given out personal information on the internet, although only 5 per cent of parents know this. And over half of them have come in contact with pornography online, with only 16 per cent of parents being aware of this.[12]

'As they get older, you've no idea what they are doing – that's quite worrying' *Clarissa, mum worried about what her boys get up to*[6]

FACT 2:

A quarter of British teenagers text message their friends more often than they talk to their families[41] and one in four 11 to 14 year olds feel that their parents don't understand them.[40]

Social overload

Symptoms: Always wanting to be in touch with the world.

 Media Alert: The constant availability of communications, emailing, texting, instant messaging, etc.

FACT 1:

Mobile phones can be stressful to kids as well as empowering. One of the biggest concerns for teenagers is 'to be constantly contactable and constantly connected to the action', according to research by The University of Bath. The research highlights the social stress which can be caused by mobile phones, with 77 per cent of the teenagers questioned agreeing with the statement 'I could not bear to be without my phone'. For many it wasn't just a question of being able to communicate, but also 'to show those around you that you are popular, successful and have a large social network.'[42]

Internet grooming

Symptoms: When an adult develops a relationship with a child over the internet – manipulating the child to trust and depend on them.

 Media Alert: Unsupervised internet chat rooms, internet dating. Kids not being aware of the dangers of the internet and being tempted by the excitement it offers.

FACT 1:

One third of 9 to 19 year olds who go online regularly have made an online acquaintance, and one in twelve say they have met face to face with someone they first met on the internet.[12]

FACT 2:

Parents generally are concerned about the risk of children forming inappropriate relationships on the internet.[6]

'My daughter, at 13, gets into content on the internet that is really inappropriate. You can chat with real people who are a lot older than you. A 13 year old is playing these online games, real time with people in their 30s.' Peter, dad of three, concerned about the dangers of the internet

5. World outlook

WORLD OUTLOOK

- Earth alien
- Bunker mentality
- Realism deficiency
- Dumbed-down values
- 'I want' culture

The media for many children is their window on the world. They see life through it and form their own judgements and values from it. The real world becomes boring because the media world seems so much more exciting. There is a risk that kids become emotionally numb. They lose the ability to enjoy simple pleasures because they are so used to the fast moving pace of the virtual world.

There is also a risk that kids acquire a distorted view of the world. They can develop perceptions of life which are at odds with reality. So, for example, they develop unfounded fears, have an upside-down sense of values, and are quick to stereotype people and emotions.

... AND IF YOU STILL NEED CONVINCING

... read the following facts and figures to stir you into action

Earth alien

Symptoms: Inability to experience pleasures of the real world – constantly needing the stimulation of the screen world. Emotionally numb when it comes to real events and relationships.

Media Alert: The media world can be so exciting – the real world can appear boring. Virtual experiences make fantasy seem like the real thing. Emotions are stretched by the TV/computer. Events are exaggerated for effect.

FACT 1:

Parents – and particularly grannies – complain that kids have lost the ability to enjoy life around them, because the virtual world is so much more enticing.[6]

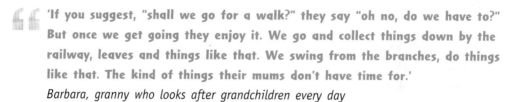 'If you suggest, "shall we go for a walk?" they say "oh no, do we have to?" But once we get going they enjoy it. We go and collect things down by the railway, leaves and things like that. We swing from the branches, do things like that. The kind of things their mums don't have time for.'
Barbara, granny who looks after grandchildren every day

And research shows that kids today are not enjoying simple pleasures in the same way their parents did. Fewer than 5 per cent of children, for instance, take part in conker fights each year.[40]

Bunker mentality

Symptoms: Feelings of anxiety about the world. Frightened about crime, preferring the haven/security of home.

 Media Alert: Violent and distorted view of the world as portrayed on TV. Overdosing on news at an early age.

FACT 1:

Parents and grandparents talk about children feeling anxious about the world around them as a result of what they've seen on TV.[6]

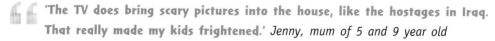 'The TV does bring scary pictures into the house, like the hostages in Iraq. That really made my kids frightened.' *Jenny, mum of 5 and 9 year old*

'Every time it rains, he asks, "Is it going to flood, gran?" It was the flooding in Boscastle that did it.' *Di, granny who looks after grandchildren once a week*

> 'When people have kidnapped other children, they always make it scary. It's really disturbing. And when the parents start talking and crying.'
> *9 year old girl*

> 'I had nightmares after the Tsunami – and I often have them after Midsommer Murders.' *8 year old girl*

Realism deficiency

Symptoms: Unable to grasp the real picture beyond the screen. Happy to live with the fantasy of an unreal world. Tendency to see things in black and white. Perceptual distortions can lead to depression, prejudice and violence.

 Media Alert: Distorted view of life through programmes and constant exposure of celebrities. Simplistic view of the world as shown on TV/computers where people are either good or bad.

FACT 1:

There is a syndrome called 'Beckham Syndrome', where teenagers believe there is no link between what they achieve at school and their potential to succeed. Research carried out on behalf of the South West Learning and Skills Council, found that 40 per cent of teenagers suffer from this syndrome. The cause has been put down to the stream of instant fame programmes such as Pop Idol and Fame Academy, and the constant exposure of football stars and TV celebrities in the media.[43]

FACT 2:

Parents and grandparents are conscious of how celebrity shows have become such an important part of their children's lives.[6]

> 'They're ordinary people and they're made out to be something fantastic and the youngsters cling on to them.' *Grandmother with five grandchildren, 5 to 15*

Dumbed-down values

Symptoms: Taking on values and perceptions of society that are at odds with your own values as a parent.

Media Alert: The constant tide of programmes/games that dramatise bad behaviour, and that portray a cool culture where anything goes.

FACT 1:

Parents are worried about the sheer quantity of 'bad behaviour' material on TV and in computer games, because they believe it affects their children's values.[6]

> 'It's dreadful because they can't think for themselves. A lot of it's bad, yes, violence plays a big part, and with the boys especially.'
> *Grandmother with five grandchildren*

Parents describe how kids can be cynical about real life because they have acquired a distorted view of the world from the screen. One mum described how her son developed the impression that policemen were the bad guys as a result of a computer game.[6]

> 'Mine played a game called Driver, where you go around in a car getting out and shooting people. It's a horrendous game. He used bad language from it, and his perceptions of the world were affected by it. He thought that the police were the bad guys, and I had to explain to him that that's not true.'
> *Liz, mum of a 7 and 10 year old*

'I want' culture

Symptoms: Wanting the latest model of everything – collecting goods like trophies – being brand-obsessed.

 Media Alert: Over-exposure to advertising. Popular culture that idolises material goods.

FACT 1:

The average child in the US sees more than 40,000 commercials each year.[44]

FACT 2:

Grannies particularly notice the prevalence of the 'I want' culture.[6]

'I want. I want. I want. What is it about children that every time you go into a shop they want everything they see. And the worst thing about my Jamie is that not only does he want it, but he somehow believes that he should get it. Nothing seems to have a true value to them. If they've seen it on TV they won't be happy till they've got it. It's exhausting.'
City granny with two grandchildren

'The "I want" culture. It's constant pressure. All the must-have games. It's got to be designer. If it's a T-shirt it's got to have a name on it.'
Barbara, granny who lives in the country

'Building up to Christmas, it's on the telly and everywhere. It's getting quite a pain. It starts far too early – it's not even November.'
Julia, who looks after her four grandchildren on weekends

For more information, go to www.mediadietforkids.com

67

So ... yes, too much is damaging

So, there is proof that too much screen time is damaging. And when you look at the character of TV and computer games it isn't surprising. Too much time sitting alone in front of a screen can't be a good thing for anyone. Or as one grandmother put it, 'Life isn't just about sitting in front of the box. If you spend hours and hours watching TV or playing on the computer, there's less time for other things.'

The message is clear ...

On the one hand, modern media can make a very positive contribution to your child's development. As we've seen, it will help them at school, boost their social life and generally enable them to make the most of life in all sorts of ways.

But at the same time, too much media is clearly damaging.

The message is clear. Modern media is great, but in moderation. So, The Media Diet isn't suggesting media starvation, but a balanced approach which gives your kid the best of all worlds.

MODERN MEDIA IS GREAT – BUT IN MODERATION

Understanding your starting point: what kind of media diet does your child need?

WHAT TYPE OF MEDIA CHILD DO I HAVE?

Focused Fred

Beware of kids with one-track minds ... they're more prone to media addiction

Macho Dude

'He's a macho dude – is he more vulnerable than his sister?'

WHAT TYPE OF MEDIA PARENT AM I?

That's a 'Battle Weary' mum

And she's 'Battle Shy'

Before you begin The Media Diet, it's useful to have a good idea of your starting point.

The two key things to look at are:

• what type of media child you have and
• what sort of media parent you are.

If you're aware of the media profiles you both have, you'll be in a better position to make the diet work. There may, for instance, be good points which you can both build on, or issues which need to be addressed.

What type of media child do I have?

How much screen media does my child consume?

The first question to ask yourself is:

"How much time is your child spending watching TV or playing computer games?"

It's important to have a rough idea of their screen time, so you know the basis from which you're starting The Media Diet.

We recommend, therefore, that before your child starts The Media Diet you make a record of their media time. An easy way of doing this is to keep a media diary. You only need to do it for a week – and it only takes a couple of minutes a day to fill in. The important thing is that you're honest with yourself – every five minutes count. It's also a good idea to make a separate note of TV and computer time so you have some idea of what the balance is.

We found from our research that the process of just completing the media diary was quite an eye opener for some parents. Time and time again parents were underestimating the time their kids were spending in front of the TV or computer. In fact, the two of us were guilty of doing this too. It wasn't until we kept a careful note that we had a clear idea of what was going on. The five minutes here and there were all adding up.

Here is the diary that we asked parents to fill in for each of their children:

THE MEDIA DIARY

Day of week	Time spent watching TV	Time spent playing computer games	Total screen time
Monday			
Tuesday			
Wednesday			
Thursday			
Friday			
Saturday			
Sunday			
Total			

Now, try it yourself. You can print off copies of The Media Diary from www.mediadietforkids.com

THE RESULTS

Here are some of the results from our research:

	Time spent watching TV	Time spent playing computer games	Total screen time
On a typical school day	2 hours	4 hours	6 hours
On a typical home day	3 hours	6 hours	9 hours

Louise aged 12

	Time spent watching TV	Time spent playing computer games	Total screen time
On a typical school day	4 hours	3 hours	7 hours
On a typical home day	4 hours	6 hours	10 hours

Iva aged 11

	Time spent watching TV	Time spent playing computer games	Total screen time
On a typical school day	4 hours	0.5 hours	4.5 hours
On a typical home day	8 hours	1 hour	9 hours

Ella aged 7

	Time spent watching TV	Time spent playing computer games	Total screen time
On a typical school day	2–3 hours	1 hour	3–4 hours
On a typical home day	4 hours	2–3 hours	6–7 hours

Shaun aged 6

Here are some comments mums made after completing The Media Diary

'Oh my God, I thought, do I let my children watch that much?'

Susie, with kids watching 8 to 10 hours on a weekend day

'I was surprised. When you put it down in black and white it suddenly seems a lot more. It's the extra few minutes here and there which all add up. It's shocking, really.'

Julia, with kids watching 4 to 6 hours on a school day

'My feelings were shock, really. I had no idea they were watching so much when I was out at work. And when I'm at home I now realise I'm using the computer and TV as a convenient entertainer and babysitter more than I thought I was.'

Paula, working mum with partner who works from home

Is my child prone to media bingeing?

Most children, if given the opportunity, can become obsessed with the screen. One of the big findings of our research, however, was that some children are more likely to over-indulge in media than others. In our own experience we've certainly found this to be true.

Louise says:

'In my case, it's Alice who is the real goggle box. She is much more focused than her older sister. I notice it with bedtime stories. Alice will listen intently while Ophelia will look around at things in the room.

So, when it comes to watching telly, Ophelia after a while will get bored and go off to do other things. Alice, on the other hand, will be gripped and could stay there for hours. It's also always Alice who'll get into a tantrum about turning it off.'

Teresa says:

'With my children it's the boys I really have to keep my eye on. They're naturally very competitive and so are always wanting to get to the next level of a computer game. And Hugo, my youngest, thinks it's particularly cool copying anything his elder brother is doing.'

A MEDIA BINGER DESCRIBES HER DAY ...

'I watch TV after school for 2 hours. Then I go on the computer for half an hour. Then I have my tea. When I've finished tea, I go on my PS2 for a few hours. Then I go to sleep with my Game Boy.'

An 8 year old girl

Just five more minutes, pleeese!

What's your kid's media profile?

The parents in our research identified different types of child who seemed to be more prone to screen addiction than others.

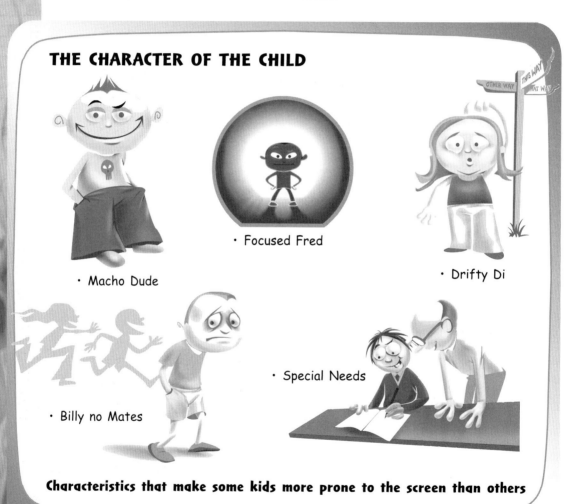

THE CHARACTER OF THE CHILD

· Macho Dude

· Focused Fred

· Drifty Di

· Billy no Mates

· Special Needs

Characteristics that make some kids more prone to the screen than others

Boy versus girl

Boys are generally more competitive than girls and, therefore, more prone to the compulsive nature of computer games. Not surprisingly, the macho imagery and aggressive action of a lot of games is particularly aimed at them.

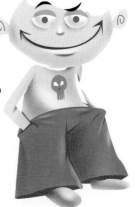

Girls tend to spend less time on computer games, although they too can become obsessed. They're more attracted to games like Sims, which is all about creating characters and situations in a fantasy world. And as they get older, girls particularly like the social dimension of the computer, such as emailing friends, visiting chat rooms and MSN.

'We've all mentioned boys, you'd never think of the girls. Girls read more, are more creative. Boys turn into men. Men like sitting and doing one thing. With women we don't want to just sit doing one thing.'
Lucinda, with two sons and a daughter

'When he was little, he had his Lego and his train, and he's not been able to replace it with anything other than the screen. He's never been particularly creative, like my girl.' *Katie with 12 year old boy*

One-track minded

Kids who enjoy working to a single goal and are very focused lose track of time when they are playing computer games. A lot of the computer games for children under 12-years-old are 'one dimensional'. You have to keep focused on one task. Again, boys tend to be more singular in their purpose, while girls are more easily bored and can feel constrained by the singular character of these games.

'He's a very focused, competitive child. He's hooked. He's like a junkie who has to have a fix.' *Cheryl, with son who's mad on computer games*

'I think the addicts fall into two categories – the rather compulsive types, or the other extreme, the less enterprising child who is lazy.'
Sarah, with two boys and two girls

Needs direction

Kids who are less motivated or resourceful can be more prone to screen addiction. TV and computer games tend to offer kids everything on a plate, so they can particularly appeal to children who are less good at tapping into their own inner resourcefulness. The screen also particularly appeals to kids who are at a loss by themselves, and are less good at playing on their own.

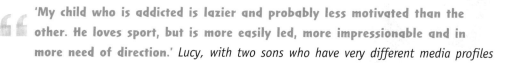

'My child who is addicted is lazier and probably less motivated than the other. He loves sport, but is more easily led, more impressionable and in more need of direction.' *Lucy, with two sons who have very different media profiles*

'Tom has to play games with people, so if there's nobody to play with, he turns to the telly. Whereas my older boy, he likes reading and enjoys time to think. Basically, he likes his own space and some peace and quiet.'
Hilary, with a yonger son who is more prone to media addiction

Solitary characters

In particular, kids who enjoy their own company and are happy to spend hours in front of the screen, rather than playing with friends.

'I think addiction is worse with kids who don't have a lot of friends. Shy kids. Only children.' *Jane, with two kids aged 7 and 9*

'I've noticed people who go to the telly are quite shy. If you're out and about, you have things to talk about. You're much more confident.' *12-year-old girl*

Special needs

Computers offer an important outlet for kids who don't do well at school. For example, kids with fine motor skill problems that lead to slow writing development. If school is a challenge, children will find comfort from their success on computer games.

'I've got a lot of kids with learning difficulties who do seem to be more computer orientated than others. It's not surprising, really. They can often do well on the computer whereas they find things like reading and writing more difficult. It makes them feel good.' *Special needs teacher*

What's your home environment?

THE HOME ENVIRONMENT

- Confined indoors

- Spend a lot of time alone

- Time-pressed parents

- Experiencing an unsettling period – eg. divorce, death, bullying

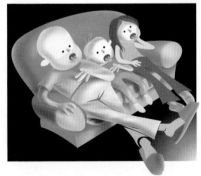

- Shuffled between parents

- Media-bingeing parents/Parents who don't have high expectations

 Characteristics that make some kids more prone to the screen than others

Many parents were quick to point out that children in certain home environments were also more prone to media bingeing than others. You only need to look at your own circle of family and friends to realise this is true. The home environment is important and has a direct influence on a child's media habits.

Children are more likely to become addicted to the screen if:

Their parents are very time-pressed

For example, families where both parents work or where there is a single parent. Or, it might simply be a family where the parents – for whatever reason – don't spend a lot of time with their children.

 'Instead of having a nanny, he's put in front of the telly. He's an only child. Both parents work, and mum works from home. She always has something to finish off.' Charlotte, carer, talking about the family next door

They have media-bingeing parents

The importance of leading by example cannot be underestimated. Kids see their parents watching loads of TV and don't understand why they should behave any differently.

 'Parents are very quick to moan that their kids are watching too much TV. But then when you look at some of the parents, it's not that surprising. Kids copy what they see. And if their parents are spending hours in front of the box, they think it's an OK thing to do. Parents have got to try and set a good example.' Head Teacher

They have parents who don't have high expectations for them

Parents with high expectations for their children are more concerned that they don't spend too much time in front of the screen. Instead, they encourage them to read and do other things away from the screen. Educated parents are also more likely to want to retain control over screen consumption. Children of educated parents are less likely to have their own TV and video, and more likely to have their own books.[45]

Children also believe you need to limit screen time if you want to have high aspirations in life.

'I wouldn't want my child just to play games all their lives. They won't get a good job. They won't be able to concentrate.' *12 year old boy*

They are confined indoors

Children who don't have easy access to outdoor space where they can play – a garden, park, safe street or open countryside – and so end up spending lots of time indoors.

Louise says:

'I don't have a garden for the kids to run around in and it does make it more difficult to entertain them. We also don't have a lot of space at home so I try and keep it all as tidy as possible. As a result, sometimes, after I've tidied up everywhere, I find myself putting the girls in front of the TV just so they don't mess it up again. It's not always the best thing for them, but it helps me out at the time.'

'It depends where you live. If you live in a city, in a tower block, your child can't really go out and play. They're going to watch more TV.'
Kim, mother from a council estate

'Even with the 15 year old I'm thinking I'd rather they were in watching DVDs. Then I know where they are.' *Karen, mother from inner city area*

'You used to be able to go anywhere. We never locked doors. Children could go up the road. Now you don't let them out of your door. You can't trust anybody.' *Carol, grandmother living in the country*

They are shuffled between separated parents

If children are regularly split between parents, it is often more difficult to keep the status quo and maintain a disciplined routine.

'I'm divorced. When they go round to his place, my 'ex' takes the box and they spend a lot of time playing on the computer.'
Sally Anne, single mum with ex-partner who takes kids at the weekend

They spend a lot of time alone

Only children, children with siblings who are much older or younger, and latchkey children who return from school to an empty home, can be vulnerable to screen addiction. These children may use the TV and computer as substitute playmates.

> 'I think it's being on his own. He can't think of anything else to do – however much you motivate him. He needs a companion and he doesn't see it in his sister who's much older than him.' *Dawn, with kids aged 7 and 12*

They're experiencing an unsettling period

This could be any one of a number of things, for example, a death or a new baby in the family, parents separating, bullying or general unhappiness at school. The screen can offer comfort and a form of escape. It can also make kids feel cool at school because they're 'in' with the playground chatter.

> 'I think he missed his father greatly. It was his way of identifying with a masculine world, while his dad wasn't there to say "let's go and kick a ball about". It was a way of finding some male imagery.
> *Sheila, granny with daughter recently separated from her partner*

> 'I have a friend who doesn't get on with her stepdad and stuff. She really likes her dad, then he left and this man came. The mum feels bad, so she gives them their own TVs upstairs, so they're not all fighting downstairs.'
> *11 year old girl*

What are the biggest 'addiction threats' to my child?

We found from our research that some media presents more of an 'addiction threat' than other media.

Computer threats

The 'big enemy' – as far as the parents we interviewed were concerned – is the computer game. Most parents thought it was more difficult to control their kids' relationship with the computer – particularly computer games – than the television.

When you look at the nature of computer games, it isn't surprising. They are designed to be addictive. There's always a reason to go back to them – to achieve a higher score, get to the next level, finish a race faster, or just do something better. Some games, however, are less addictive than others. FIFA and Gran Turismo, for instance, are easier to walk away from because you play a match or drive a race. After that it's finished. If you want to continue you have to start again.

Teresa says:

'I had a good glimpse of this the other day. My son Chris became totally obsessed by his new computer game – Medal of Honor. It's a type of war game and he managed to get to level 3. He was thrilled. The following day, he woke up and all he wanted to do was to get to the next level. He became obsessed. Drastic action was needed. I needed to clear his mind and so I took him off on a bike ride. It did the trick. He was thinking and talking about other things when we got back.'

MSN is also becoming a big headache for parents – particularly those with daughters. It's great for kids because it's so social but it can quickly become addictive – and very time consuming. If kids know their friends are online it is difficult not to join in the chatter.

(See separate section on MSN pages 147–149)

85

Parents say:

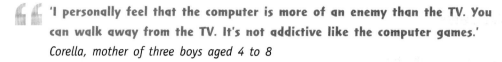

'I personally feel that the computer is more of an enemy than the TV. You can walk away from the TV. It's not addictive like the computer games.' *Corella, mother of three boys aged 4 to 8*

'With computers there's always just something else, whereas with the TV, it's finished'. *Katherine, with three children aged 5 to 10*

'Games are interactive, competitive. You have to win. They're more aggressive. Lots of things are happening on the screen which make you very jumpy. He's in there on that screen. Whereas when he's watching TV he just sits back and absorbs what's going on.' *Sandra, with a son and daughter aged 5 and 8*

Kids say:

'Even after four hours I want to play more. You get addicted to it. You do one bit and you just want to carry on.' *11 year old boy*

'You know you can do it, but you can't do it.' *12 year old boy*

'One of the war games I play is very addictive, because you can't save the games so you have to carry on until you've finished.' *10 year old boy*

Television threats

When it comes to television, parents pointed out a number of specific problem areas. One was television soaps which can become obsessive viewing for 9 to 12 year old girls. They love the story lines, the characters and that sense of escapism.

Another area mentioned was the cartoon channels. These appeal mostly to kids between 5 to 8 years old, who become mesmerised by the imagery and fast action of the cartoon world. A problem often arises in homes which have recently acquired digital channels. The sudden availability of cartoons 24 hours a day is just too good to be true. It can take a little time for things to settle down in these homes. In some cases the problem persists and the kids remain hooked.

And of course, there is sport on TV. In homes where there are football-mad dads, it can be very difficult for mums to draw anyone away from the box when she thinks they've had enough.

How can I tell if my child is addicted to the screen?

There's no scientific formula to tell whether a child is, or isn't, a 'media addict'.

But there are questions which you can ask yourself if you're worried your child is becoming too dependent on the screen. We've compiled a 'Media Addiction Check List' (see overleaf). If you find that most of the answers to these questions are 'yes', your child isn't necessarily addicted, but you should certainly watch the situation closely.

You'll also need to be particularly sensitive about how you approach the diet itself. For instance, rather than adopting it all at once, you may decide to take a more gradual approach and do it in stages.

> **'I think it's a problem when it's all they're thinking of.'**
> *Tracey, mum with children who have been media-addicted in the past*

> **'I've seen a five year old get out of the bed in the mornings and go straight on to the Game Boy. He was obviously addicted.'**
> *Teacher and mum, concerned about the dangers of early morning game play*

> **'It happened without us realising. He'd be on the computer a bit more every day. And now it's difficult to stop. He becomes very aggressive when I try and get him off. I think we're going to have to get rid of the thing altogether.'** *Jacky, mum concerned about her 8 year old son's behaviour*

MEDIA ADDICTION CHECK LIST

Six Key Questions for Parents to ask: Yes No

1. Is watching the TV or playing the computer the first thing your child wants to do in the morning?

2. Would your child generally prefer to be alone in front of the screen rather than doing things with friends or family?

3. Is your child particularly depressed when he or she comes away from the screen?

4. Does he or she seem to be thinking of the screen most of the time?

5. Is your child 'screen blinkered' – in other words, can he or she focus on anything other than screen-based activity? Does he or she have difficulty completing any non-screen based activity?

6. Does he need the television or computer before he goes to sleep at night?

Remember, if most of your answers are 'yes', your child is not necessarily addicted but you should watch the situation carefully.

 Fill in the chart, or get a copy from www.mediadietforkids.com

Chapter 4

What type of media parent are you?

What's your media outlook?

And now, let's turn to you – the parent. We discovered from our research a range of attitudes amongst parents to the screen.

The Screen Rules OK!

At one end of the spectrum there are parents with their heads buried firmly in the sand. As far as they're concerned 'the screen rules OK!' Basically, anything goes. These parents seem resigned to the fact that the media should dominate their children's lives and just see it as a sign of the times.

Children in these households are consuming up to or more than 10 hours of television and computer time on days when they're at home, and over 5 hours on school days.

The Tight Controllers

At the other extreme are the Tight Controllers. These parents have strict media regimes for their kids and don't regard media control in their homes as a problem. The children of these parents are typically spending less than one hour a day in front of the screen.

In between these two extremes, we found two types of 'concerned' parents.

The Battle Shy

The first are the Battle Shy. In these cases the 'screen rules' but parents are uneasy and feel guilty about it. They would rather the TV or computer games remain on, than have a confrontation with their children. Children in these homes are watching up to eight hours a day on a home day.

The Battle Weary

The second are the Battle Weary. These parents are controlling the screen but with growing difficulty. For them it is a constant battle to keep their children's screen time down. On a home day these kids are spending anything from a couple of hours to up to five or six hours at the screen.

In both these last two cases, the screen provokes a mixture of positive and negative feelings. But Battle Shy and Battle Weary parents have one important thing in common – they all want help with controlling their children's screen time.

So, what type of mum or dad are you?

Teresa says:

'I was feeling very Battle Weary when we started writing this book. At 6 and 9 years my two boys are at prime ages to become computer game addicts. With Isabel it's been more a problem of working out what rules should apply for her use of the internet and MSN. As a mum I have been struggling to keep things in control and have valued exchanging tips with other mums coping with the same pressures. And yes, testing out the principles of The Media Diet has been helpful – it has given me and the kids a new set of ground rules to work from.'

Louise says:

'I am a Tight Controller – but not as much as I thought I was. The Media Diary was very revealing. It made me realize that the children were spending more time in front of the telly than I thought.

There are lots of times when I feel Battle Weary but I realise I've got it relatively easy – at the moment – because my kids are still quite young.

I'm very conscious, however, that things will change. I've noticed friends who seemed to have it all under control when their kids were the same age as mine, and who now seem less comfortable with how they're controlling the screen at home. I'm in danger of becoming a Battle Weary mum because I'm not as good at saying "no" as I should be. Even now with Alice – aged only 2 – I sometimes find it hard to resist her pleas to turn the telly on.'

WHAT TYPE OF PARENT ARE YOU?

'Screen rules Ok'
It's the way of today

'Battle Shy'
I'm out of control - and I feel bad about it

'Battle Weary'
It's a constant battle trying to keep in control

'Tight Controller'
I'm in control - so this isn't my problem

If you're one of those parents who is Battle Shy or Battle Weary, then you're half way there. You've identified something's not quite right. You're aware that your kids are spending too much time in front of the screen but you're not quite sure what to do about it. You're psychologically prepared. The Media Diet provides you with the simple solution you've probably been looking for.

If you're a Screen Rules OK parent, you obviously need more convincing. We came across some parents in our research who had been relaxed about the amount of time their children were spending in front of the TV or computer. But then something suddenly snapped and they decided to do something about it.

In one case it was a dad who realised his son was spending so much time in front of the computer that he had become introvert and didn't even want to see his friends. The only way the father could deal with the situation was to get rid of the computer. He went from one extreme to another. It's much better to take control of the situation now, rather than having to resort to such drastic action at a later stage.

And finally, you may be the Tight Controller. If so, that's great. You're already in control of your child's media time. You now just need to make sure that you're making the most of everything that modern media can offer.

What the Screen Rules OK mums told us:

'That's what they want to do. I think they get enough pressure. So why can't they chill out and do what they want?' *Anna, mum on inner-city estate*

'I accept it because it is a way of life.' *Sharon, working professional mum*

Battle Shy:

'Oh my God, I thought, do I let them watch that much?'
Jasmine, mum with kids in front of the screen for about 8 hours on the weekend

'I was quite surprised. It's quite convenient if you're doing something, and that quite shocked me.' *Jennie, mum busy juggling a part-time job from home*

Battle Weary:

'I have big problems with my second son because he just wants to play with other kids. If no one is available to play, he just turns the telly on. I do find it an endless battle to get him away.'
Caroline, mum having difficulties with her second son

'I find it really difficult in the winter. In the summer they'd rather be kicking a football about. In the winter it's so hard getting them off the computer and TV.' *Jemma, mum with two boys and a 2 year old girl*

'The biggest problem is that it involves much more time from the parents. I've always got something to do, like cook the tea. I try to encourage them to do other things, but I never seem to have enough time.'
Angela, mum juggling part-time job and kids

Tight Controller:

'I'm a control freak. I have a points system where the boys can earn points and then stars. They can then 'buy' special treats. So, it might be 10 minutes of a TV programme – or something completely different, like a chocolate bar. But then it all gets too complicated and it goes pear-shaped. I can't work out who's owed what, and I just cave in.' *Melissa, mum of 8 year old twin boys*

'We have a PlayStation, but we only play with it on Saturday afternoon, and I limit it to 45 minutes.' *Liz, mum living in rural village*

'They only watch the telly on a Friday and weekends. Basically there's no time by the time they've done their homework.' *Claire, nanny with firm rules*

And are you ...
... a dad or a mum?

We found a big difference between mums and dads when it comes to kids and the media – particularly with computer games.

At the risk of sounding sexist, we are going to make a few generalisations here – obviously there are always exceptions to every rule. But, in our research we found that dads tend to see everything about computers in haloed terms, whereas mums naturally are more worried about the dangers of computer games.

So, dads are usually:

More media-savvy

It's dad who gets kids started on new games and fixes problems.

'I'm the computer Mr Fix-it. It can be a real bore at times.' *Andrew, accountant*

'She always asks her dad because he is far more clever than me with the computer.' *Susan, at-home mum with two girls aged 8 and 13 years old*

More happy to join in

Dads are the ones who are more likely to play computer games with their children.

 'My brother and I play a lot with my boys. We've got a six player football game. It's a great social thing. It's very complicated, three on each side, but we're good at it.' *Hugh, sales executive*

More time-indulgent

Dads are less worried than mums about the amount of time kids spend on the computer, and more likely to point out the positive benefits.

 'Everyone moans about how kids plonk themselves down, but computer games are good for eye and hand coordination.' *Nigel, taxi driver*

More inclined to spoil

It's often dad who buys the new games – because he wants to play them too.

 'Our kids tend to save up and buy their own games. Unless it's something I really want, then I get it. I counted we have 39 games. The other day I bought San Andreas for my big boys. It's amazing.' *Neil, garage mechanic*

More inclined to watch lots of sport

When it comes to TV, the big difference between mums and dads is sport. Here again, this can cause problems for mums who want to limit TV viewing. It's difficult for a mum to get kids away from the screen, if dad remains glued to it.

 'We have sport on every night. My boys watch it every night with my partner. There's nothing I can do. My partner decides.'
Nikki, at-home mum with sport-loving partner

Less worried about violence and adult content

Dads seem to be generally more relaxed about what boys are exposed to on the telly or computer. *Let them discover it for themselves*, was the general view of a lot of the dads we spoke to.

'Mum would say, "No, you're not having that because there's too much swearing". Then my dad would get it.' *12 year old boy*

'My dad would buy me an 18, but my mum wouldn't. We hide it. She found one and put it in the bin.' *11 year old boy*

'Let them discover it for themselves. Don't shroud them too much.'
Chris, relaxed dad, truck driver

... except when it comes to their daughters

In contrast, dads are very protective over their daughters. A typical example of this was one dad who was very happy for his son to play games like Grand Theft Auto: San Andreas, but was much more cautious about what he would let his daughter get up to.

'Sex is getting to their brains. With San Andreas you can do a lot more. You can pick up the prostitutes and you get them into the car and you hear it all. And there's lots more blood and destruction. Yes, it's OK for my 13 year old boy, but not the girl. I'm protective of girls, even when she's 14 or 15 I wouldn't want her to play it.'
Neil, garage mechanic with 13 year old boy and 11 year old girl

With dads so enthusiastic about television and computer games, it can make it difficult for mums to try and limit screen time. So, if you're a dad, keep up the good work enthusing kids about the wonders of modern media. But make sure you're sensitive to the downsides. If mum is trying to limit the kids' screen time, look at how you can work with her as a team.

And mums, stick to your instincts. Don't be afraid to stand up to dad and the kids, if you feel they've had their quota of screen time. But try and make sure you don't get left in the dark. Take some time out occasionally to play computer games with your child.

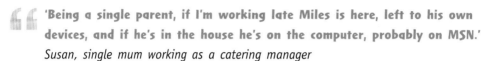

... And are you ...
... a single parent?

Are things different if you're a single mum or dad? Of course, they are. With two parents about it makes sense to work as a team: 'you do the school reading while I make tea'; 'you do the supermarket shop while I go to the playground'.

❝ **'Being a single parent, if I'm working late Miles is here, left to his own devices, and if he's in the house he's on the computer, probably on MSN.'**
Susan, single mum working as a catering manager

❝ **'He went through a stage when he wouldn't even go to Sainsbury's without his Game Boy. Dad wasn't there to say, put it down, let's go and hit a football.'**
Sheila, granny of a boy, whose daughter had recently separated from her partner

When you have to do it all on your own, it's twice as difficult to fit everything into the day. The TV and computer can play a very important role in helping entertain kids. This is particularly true of single parents who are full-time workers.

Single parents spoke about the difficulty of arranging social events for their children, and the positive way that computers can keep kids in touch and socially engaged.

MSN was the chat forum that was mentioned the most. Parents had mixed views about it. On the one hand it allows a child to be sociable, but it also becomes very addictive. One single mum described her 13 year old son who had over 50 contacts in his address book. She had to limit his MSN chatter time to 2 hours each night.

❝ **'He'd be on MSN for 6 hours – if I didn't limit him. It's all love talk with his mates. At least it means he's on the computer talking to his friends. It's difficult as a single mum taking him all around the country to be with friends.'** *Susan, single mum with 12 year old son*

We didn't find that children with single parents were necessarily more glued to the screen than other kids. But obviously if you're on your own, it can be that much harder to get the balance right.

... And are you ...
... a working mum?

Children with working parents – particularly working mums – are more prone to media bingeing. It's easy to understand why. For a start, mum may not be there when the kids get home so it's not surprising that kids just flop in front of the telly.

'If I'm working late he's in the house alone, and he will be on the computer and MSN. But at least I know he's safe, I don't want him outside. It is difficult. I'm stuck in a full-time job. Children do get left to themselves.'
Barbara, single mum in a full-time job

One mum of a 12 year old girl described how her girl lets herself in:

'3 times a week I'm not there when she comes back. Then she might turn the telly on.' *Fay, part-time working mum*

Then when mum returns she is often too tired to think of anything apart from the next chore to be done. Encouraging the children away from the screen is a low priority.

And this is where we need to put our hands in the air. We're two working mums who rely on modern media to help us get by. Yes, we use the TV to entertain the kids if we're exhausted after a day's work – or even to distract them for the odd half hour or so, if there's still work to be done.

We talked to carers who described exhausted mums returning from work, too tired to do anything. In some homes we found friction between parents and carers about how to control the TV and computer games. Carers often felt frustrated. They would enforce certain rules during the week, only to find that everything went out of the window when the parents were in charge in the evening and at the weekend.

> 'On the weekend they watch masses of telly with their parents. It can make it difficult because I become the nasty one, always saying no.'
> Jenny, nanny looking after kids of two professional parents

Parents, on the other hand, were sometimes worried that carers were using the telly more than they should to make their job easier. But in other homes, we found parents and carers were working together well. They had agreed rules regarding the computer and the TV, and stuck by them.

THEN WHEN MUM RETURNS SHE IS OFTEN TOO TIRED TO THINK OF ANYTHING APART FROM THE NEXT CHORE ...

... And are you ...
.... separated from your partner?

With split-up and divorced parents there is often the problem of a lack of consistency between parents. So, for example, a mum might have certain rules for the TV and computer, but as soon as the kids visit their dad everything goes out of the window.

We also found that separated parents can be more likely to over-indulge their children. It's natural. If you're only with your child for a limited amount of time, you want to get on with them. You don't particularly want a confrontation about whether or not to turn off the telly.

> **'Monique doesn't see her dad much so it's special. He doesn't want her not to enjoy it. He doesn't seem to mind her being on the computer all the time. But he does comment that he never sees her any more. She's in one room on the computer and he's in the front room.'** *Sharon, divorced mum*

So, the big message here is that although you may be separated, try and work together as a team. And – if you can – don't be tempted to over-indulge your kids.

And just remember ... you're not alone

One final thought before we go on to the diet. If you're struggling to get the right media balance in your child's life, just remember ... you're not alone.

The grandparents in our research identified four big changes in the world today, that they believe make it more difficult to control the use of media at home.

Why it's so hard now

Shortage of time

The biggest change was a shortage of time. Mums today, they said, are generally much more pushed for time than they used to be. And they're right. There are many more working mums and the pace of life is more hectic than ever.

'So many of our daughters work. My daughter is a single mum. It's so tempting just to plonk them in front of the telly.' *Evelyn, granny with four grandchildren*

Our children's lack of freedom

The second change they identified was the lack of freedom we give our children. Again, it's true. We kept on coming across parents who were worried about their children's safety outside the home. And who can blame them? For these parents, the option of their children spending hours in front of the screen was often far better than having them playing unsupervised outside.

'Some people are frightened to death to let their children out. My 10 year old, I don't even want her riding her bike up and down the street. Whether it's good or bad, I'd rather her inside watching videos. It's all the paedophiles and things.' *Deborah, mother from inner-city area*

It's harder to say 'No'

Thirdly, the grandparents talked about the problem of parents who can't say 'no'. Most of us are probably guilty of over-indulging our children. Grandparents certainly think we do.

'There's not so much discipline as there used to be. "I want, I want, I want" all the time. Parents say "yes" rather than "no – unless it's your birthday or you save up for it".' *Ellen, who looks after her grandchildren after school*

There's so much of it about!

And finally, of course, they identified the proliferation of new media. In the old days there were a limited number of channels and programmes to choose from. But today there is 24-hour coverage. Anyone can watch almost anything, at any time of day.

'I pity any mum trying to control the telly. In our day it was simple. There wasn't much choice. Now it's everywhere. How do you stop it when it's all around you?' *Joan, grandmother of six, aged between 3 and 15*

'It's like trying to get someone to cut down on sweets if they worked in a chocolate factory. The media's everywhere. Of course our kids are addicted.' *Kim, mother of three aged 6–10*

IT'S NOT HOW IT USED TO BE!

- Parents have less time
- Children have less freedom
- There's more pressure on parents to indulge children
- There's such a proliferation of media

Hopefully, a lot of what we've covered in this section sounds familiar.

You should now be mentally prepared for the diet. You know what type of media parent you are – a Tight Controller, Screen Rules OK or something in between. You should also have a good idea of the kind of media consumer your child is. And there may be particular media issues you've spotted which need to be handled with care.

Now, all that's left to do is to get going – to try out The Media Diet itself.

The Media Diet — a 3-step solution

THE 3-STEP MEDIA DIET

Step 1: From calorie counting to time counting

- how to set limits for TV and computer games
- how to keep to the limits – the 7 Golden Rules

Step 2: From junk programming to healthy media

- how to become a media-savvy parent
- how to raise a media-savvy child

Step 3: From media addiction to media substitutes

- encouraging activity away from the screen
- Our Recipe – 6 ingredients for time away from the screen

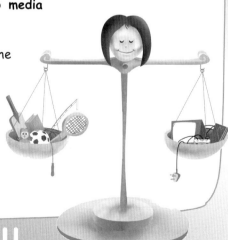

From calorie counting to time counting

It's time to set a limit

STEP 1 – SETTING LIMITS

... FROM CALORIE COUNTING TO TIME COUNTING

- how to set limits for TV and Computer Games

- how to keep to the limits – the 7 Golden Rules

- problems and solutions

How to set limits for TV and computer games

The first step of The Media Diet is all about cutting down on media consumption. But how much time is too much time? Although there is general agreement that our children are overdosing on too much screen media, up until recently few people have been prepared to say what the limit should be. We believe that it's now time for parents to set a limit.

The Media Diet recommends that you aim for less than 2 hours as your child's average daily limit for 'screen entertainment'. The reason why we believe the figure '2' is so important is explained on the following pages.

You mustn't worry about being too exact. Think of the figure 2 as a rule of thumb – your child may come in well below it, or even above it. The most important thing is that you have a figure to aim for.

RULE OF THUMB

What is 'screen entertainment'?

First of all, what do we mean by the 'screen'?

In the majority of homes the television and computer are treated as two different types of activity. Children start off the evening watching telly, and then migrate seamlessly from it to the computer and back to the telly again. As far as their parents are concerned, it's a separate thing. So, it's either telly time or computer time.

107

The fact that a lot of us think like that isn't surprising. In the past, we would watch the television and play or work on the computer. But today you can use your television to play games or go shopping. And you can watch films or listen to your favourite music on the computer. In short, it's becoming harder to distinguish between the two.

The Media Diet treats television and computer screen activity as one. We've done this for a number of reasons:

1. The merging together of computer and television technology means that they share more and more of the same characteristics. And this trend will continue in the future.

2. People may describe the TV as passive and the computer as interactive, but the similarities are great. Both tend to be sedentary activities and most importantly, a child's fantasies and imagination are constrained by the images on the screen.

3. Time spent on the computer or watching television, means time *not* spent doing other things. If you want a healthy balance in your child's life there needs to be a good mixture of screen and non screen activity.

So, that's what we mean by the 'screen'. What then, do we mean by 'screen *entertainment*'?

When we say screen entertainment – we mean *entertainment*. We do not, for example, mean to limit your child from using the computer for educational and creative purposes. It is the screen as entertainer that has become so addictive – and it is this entertainment, be it passive TV or interactive games that needs controlling.

More specifically, 'screen entertainment' does not include any activity where your child is:

Doing research

Taking the initiative and using media for specific research tasks, such as using the internet to investigate a specific subject for pleasure or for homework. Internet research has become an important part of the National Curriculum, and it is important that kids develop these research skills for adult life.

Being creative

Using the computer as a medium for creativity – just as a writer or an artist uses a blank sheet of paper. In these situations children have to dig deep into their own creative resources. Kids are initiating the ideas and simply using the computer as a word or creative processor.

Contacting friends

Making contact with friends. This is territory where a parent needs to keep a close eye on their child. We believe that it is good to encourage children to use email, texting and MSN in moderation. However, if a child shows signs of spending obsessive lengths of time on them, then we suggest that parents should set limits (*see separate note on MSN on pages 147–149*).

Learning and exercise

Using the screen for specific educational or exercise roles, such as educational games, language learning or dancing. When a child is using the screen as a means of independent learning – as support for school work or simply for pleasure – this is obviously an activity that should be valued and encouraged.

The 2-hour time limit

As we said at the start of the chapter, The Media Diet recommends that you aim for less than 2 hours as your child's average daily limit for 'screen entertainment'. The limit of 2 hours is a figure we chose for a number of reasons.

As one of the country's leading children's researchers Teresa has been studying the impact of modern media on children for the last twenty years. In particular, she has followed the effects that too much media exposure can have on a child's development. She believes the limit of 2 is the right figure.

Her views are supported by a new wave of research studies which confirm that too much screen time is a real threat – and, for example, that over 2 hours' TV a day can damage a child for life. The figure of 2 is in line with leading children and health experts. The American Academy of Pediatrics, for instance, recommend that children should watch no more than two hours of television a day.[46]

And – very importantly – it's a figure that felt right to mums. As two mums ourselves we felt we could live with it and keep to it. And when we tried it out on other mums and dads they felt the same. Most of the people we interviewed felt that the 2 hour limit achieved the right balance. It's low enough to protect children from the dangers of too much media exposure. But it's not high enough to stop kids benefiting from everything that the modern media world has to offer.

Don't panic if 2 seems impossible

But if the target of '2' feels too ambitious, don't panic. The Media Diary (*see page 74*) will have given you an idea of your child's current media consumption. If his or her screen time is considerably more than two hours a day, and you feel uncomfortable about aiming for 2 straightaway, there are a number of options to consider.

1. Stagger your approach

It's important to set yourself realistic targets. So, decide what time limit feels comfortable for you and your child. If, for instance, your child is currently spending five hours a day in front of the screen, you might decide to aim for four hours in the first month, three in the second and two in the third.

'We did have a problem with our daughter watching too much telly. We managed to sort it out with a softly, softly approach. She's quite stubborn and so anything else she would have rebelled against. We started gradually limiting the amount of time she could spend in front of the TV until we got it down to a level we were happy with. It didn't become a big issue because we did it slowly.' *Bob, dad of one daughter, aged 8*

'The limit should depend on what they're used to. If they're used to 10 hours, then make it 4, then 2. Then you can get it gradually down.' *11 year old girl*

2. Wait for the right moment – if now's not a good time

A good time to start any diet is when there's a natural change in circumstances or routine. Another change – like the diet itself – somehow doesn't then seem such a big deal. So you might want, for instance, to wait until the beginning of the school holidays, or start of a new term, to begin the diet.

'We could never find the right day to start cutting back on the TV. There was always some reason why not to do it – the kids had friends round, it was raining or there was something special to watch. In the end we decided to take the plunge after we'd come back from our summer holidays. They were out of their normal routine and so it was easier to kick their old habits.' *Anna, mum of three kids aged 6, 8 and 12*

3. Go 'Cold Turkey'

Some parents find the easiest way of regaining control is to take drastic action. They get rid of the TV and computer altogether and then have a fresh start. This approach is particularly popular with parents of children who were spending excessive amounts of time in front of the screen.

If you decide to go down this route, make sure that your child understands that it is only for a limited period. You also need to have plenty of ideas and activities lined up for your child to fill the void once the TV or computer is switched off. And once you do bring the TV and computer back, make sure it is done on your own terms.

> 'Our son is 8 and became totally obsessed by his computer games. The only way we could do anything about it was to get rid of the computer altogether. We did try limiting his time but it didn't seem to work. Because it was still there he would keep on nagging me to switch it on. Once he saw it had gone he knew we were serious. After a while we brought it back – but with new rules. He seems to respect the rules now – mainly because he knows if he breaks them it will go again.' *Fiona, mum of three kids*

> 'She banned the PlayStation for a week.'
> *12 year old boy whose mum had given up negotiating*

> 'She took my PlayStation away, and didn't give it back until I pleaded and pleaded.' *12 year old boy whose mum went tough, and then relented*

What do we mean by 'a daily average'?

The Media Diet is designed to be flexible so that it can easily fit into your family's lifestyle. Not every day is the same. Your children's needs differ from day to day, and from week to week.

The figure of 2 hours, therefore, is an average across the year.

How does this work in practice? Well, take a school day, for instance. If you're anything like us, there's never enough time to cram everything in. The kids get back from school. They've got to be fed. They need to relax. They want to play. There's homework to be done. And before you know it, it's time for bed.

The weekend is a different ball game altogether. There's lots of time to fill. It's also a time to relax and chill out. So, you might decide to aim for '1' hour screen time on a school day, and '3' for a home day. It will average out roughly, so you're still achieving that magic '2'. Or, perhaps, you'll go for 1½ hours during the week and 2½ hours at the weekend. It's up to you.

Likewise, the weather is an important factor. If it's pouring with rain and you've nowhere to go, some extra screen time is probably going to keep the whole family sane. But, if it's a beautiful day – don't waste it! Save up those 'media hours' for another day. Get the kids outside enjoying the weather. Again, just make sure that it averages out roughly at no more than 2 hours screen time a day.

The Media Clock emerged from our research as a useful device to allocate media time. It helps you decide how to spread your children's screen entertainment hours across the year. It shows you how you can vary their media consumption according to different days. The clock below, for instance, allocates 1–2 hours for a rainy school day and 2–3 hours for a sunny home day.

THE MEDIA CLOCK

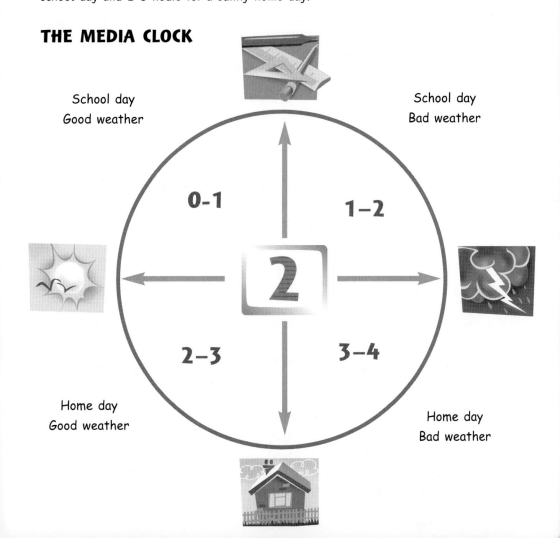

School day
Good weather

School day
Bad weather

0-1

1–2

2

2–3

3–4

Home day
Good weather

Home day
Bad weather

THE MEDIA CLOCK

School day
Good weather

School day
Bad weather

Home day
Good weather

Home day
Bad weather

Here's a blank Media Clock to fill in. Decide with your child what figures to aim for. For more copies of The Media Clock, go to www.mediadietforkids.com

Does the 2-hour limit apply to all ages?

The Media Diet is for 2 to 12 year olds. The two hour limit, therefore, is aimed at all children within this age range. But a certain degree of flexibility is also important. The demands and needs of a 2 year old are – of course – very different to those of a 12 year old. So, at times you might find yourself being more indulgent to a particular child, because of their age and stage in life, than another. That's fine. Go with it.

Be sensitive to your child and where they're coming from ... while trying to keep half an eye on their media clock. And remember that kids look to you as their role models. So, if you're spending lots of time in front of the screen, you may want to try and keep an eye on your media clock too.

To help you along, here are a few thoughts about the different ages and what you can expect from a media perspective.

2 to 5 year olds

Enjoy it while it lasts. These kids can still be easily distracted with games or other activities away from the screen. And the problem of peer pressure hasn't yet properly kicked in.

Make the most of these early years to protect them from too much screen time. Children of this age group are growing fast and so it's important that they are given plenty of opportunities to develop basic skills like talking, interacting with others, learning how to think and solve problems. Also, if you establish good habits early on, the next stage will be that much easier.

Louise says:

'Ophelia and Alice both fall into this age group. They're still at the age where they find most things exciting, and can be distracted. They will ask to watch certain things, but mostly it's a passing whim and two seconds later they've forgotten about it.

I find that sometimes I make the mistake of being too quick to turn on the TV. I think they need to be entertained when in fact they're very happy just being left alone to explore other options.'

6 to 9 year olds

This is when it starts to get trickier and your media parenting skills will begin to be put to the test. Just when you thought you had everything under control, things change. Children are at proper school and television and computer games become the topic of playground chatter. Kids are also discovering for themselves what the media world has to offer.

Kids in this age group often benefit from some time in front of the screen just to chill out. But it's important that guidelines are set and kept to.

Teresa says:

'Hugo and Christopher are our 6 to 9 year olds. They certainly come back from school exhausted and need their chill out time in front of the TV. They have also become computer game enthusiasts and often have fun playing together. They need firm authority so I have to keep a close eye on the clock otherwise I would lose them to the screen all day.

Peer group pressure has become very important for Christopher who is 9. He often comes back from school with all the news about the latest games and DVD releases. He is always putting me under pressure to buy something, and last week it was The Incredibles DVD. I said I would wait until it came down in price ... "you always do that mum," he grumbled, and then he went on to explain that there was no point seeing films when no one was talking about them.

He is also putting me under enormous pressure to buy him 15+ and 18+ rated games. There is obviously much playground chat about the games that older brothers and dads play, and this creates a bravado amongst the kids who have access to the older rated games. It takes a lot of resolve not to succumb to his constant badgering, but at least I have the support of his dad who agrees that we should stick to the ratings guidelines.

Christopher is also beginning to use email – he is keeping in touch with a friend who has moved to Australia. But my biggest problem with him and the internet is the problem of internet shopping. He often goes on to sports sites and looks longingly at football and cricket shirts. This week he found a sweetie site that sells 'Toxic Waste' – a foul sounding sweet that is the latest craze at school. He was delighted and of course, in no time, he was on the hunt for mum and her credit card. The commercial pressures of the internet can be a constant headache for parents – particularly at this age when kids are less appreciative of the value of money.'

10 to 12 year olds

It's pressure all round – the kids have 101 things to do and they're asking you for yet more time in front of the screen. Computer game usage normally peaks amongst children aged 9 to 14 years old. Schoolwork becomes more important and homework eats into more of the evening. Kids are also often being encouraged to do lots of other activities and hobbies.

Your child is changing too. He or she has become more independent and probably more difficult to control. You have to be firm about how the TV and computer games can be used, but you also need to encourage your child to start taking some responsibility for their own media time.

Teresa says:

'Isabel falls into this category. Suddenly she seems so much more mature and is taking responsibility for her own timetable. I don't have to hound her quite so much to get started on the homework.

She has an old laptop which has a wireless connection to the internet. Somehow I feel I can trust her with this independence – but I am keeping a close eye on how she uses it. She only uses MSN and email in moderation – so I'm lucky that I don't have any battles to fight in that area. Sometimes, however, I do have problems getting her off Sims or RollerCoaster Tycoon before she goes to bed.'

So, the 2-hour limit is a guideline – but allow yourself some flexibility depending on your child's stage in life – and the mood of the moment.

Understanding why '2' is right for you

It's no point going on the diet unless you and your children understand and believe in the '2' hour limit. We recommend one way of doing this is to do a 'Time Check'.

To do this, all you have to do is prioritise the things that need to be fitted into your child's day – for example, homework, a hobby, some exercise outside and a family meal. Once you've done this you can work out how much time is left for your child to spend in front of the TV or computer. You then allocate your child's 'media time' accordingly.

The Time Check is useful because it illustrates clearly why the 2-hour limit is so important. By focusing on what ideally needs to be done in a day – and the limited hours available – you appreciate the importance of controlling your children's media time.

MEDIA TIME CHECK – SCHOOL DAY

4.00–4.30 pm	TV
4.30–5.00 pm	Outdoors
5.00–5.30 pm	Homework
5.30–6.00 pm	Eating/chat
6.00–6.30 pm	Non-screen play
6.30–7.00 pm	Computer
7.00–7.30 pm	Bath
7.30–8.00 pm	Bedtime reading

Total = 8 half-hour units

Agree your own family priorities and see what limit feels right for you

Fill in the chart below or get a copy from www.mediadietforkids.com

MEDIA TIME CHECK – SCHOOL DAY

4.00–4.30 pm	
4.30–5.00 pm	
5.00–5.30 pm	
5.30–6.00 pm	
6.00–6.30 pm	
6.30–7.00 pm	
7.00–7.30 pm	
7.30–8.00 pm	

Total = 8 half-hour units

Agree your own family priorities and see what limit feels right for you

MEDIA TIME CHECK – HOME DAY

Time slot		Home Day guidelines
Before breakfast		
Breakfast		
First half morning		
Second half morning	Computer	
Lunch		
Afternoon	TV / Computer	
Tea		
Evening	TV / TV / TV	
Bed		

Home Day guidelines

During the holidays there's no need to be too clock-bound. Just think of the day in terms of slugs of time, e.g. before breakfast, first half of morning and so forth

Now think roughly how much screen time seems right, e.g. four half units for a sunny out and about day, or eight half hour units for a wet, home-bound day

Let your kid decide where he/she spends those units of screen time. Get them to fill in their half hour media slots on the time chart

---

Isabel's Time Check (School Day)

Teresa says:

'When Isabel (12 years old) comes back from school she'll normally have half an hour in front of the television. She's often very tired and just needs to flop and recharge her batteries.

I then encourage her to go outside and get some exercise – play some netball or bicycle around the block. After this she'll have half an hour on the computer. I try and encourage computer games, like Sims, which make the most of her creativity. She then has to have a good hour for homework and piano practice.'

MEDIA TIME CHECK – HOME DAY

Before breakfast

Breakfast

First half morning

Second half morning

Lunch

Afternoon

Tea

Evening

Bed

Here's a Media Time Check for your child to fill in. For more copies go to www.mediadietforkids.com

Chris and Hugo's Time Check (Home Day)

Teresa says:

'I think of home days in terms of slugs of time. I'm not as precise as I am for school days, where every half hour is valuable time. I still, however, think of media time in terms of half hour slots.

I don't let Chris or Hugo watch too much TV in the morning because I find it leaves them soporific and demotivated. It's then difficult to get them to do anything else for the rest of the day. They might, though, have half an hour on the computer, or PlayStation, before lunch.

In the afternoon and evening – depending on what we're doing and the weather – they'll watch an hour or two of television and have half an hour on the computer.'

Ophelia and Alice's Time Check (Home Day)

Louise says:

'I find with two young children – Ophelia and Alice – it's as much a matter of when I need a bit of peace and quiet, as when they might benefit from time in front of the screen. I tend to be quite flexible and use the screen very tactically – either to give me space to do something else, to defuse those tension moments, or sometimes as a bribe to get something done.

Typically, they might watch 15 minutes of TV in the morning while I'm getting dressed. They then might watch half an hour of a video sometime after lunch. This is precious time for me to do my own thing. But if they're happily playing I don't even mention the video option to them.

I might turn the TV or a video on again when we come back from whatever we've been doing in the afternoon. This is often a stressful time because the children are hungry and tired – and there's still tea to cook. The TV just calms them down and buys me a few moments peace. And then the video often goes on again for half an hour after their bath and before story time.

There are other times when I simply turn on the video or TV because I urgently need ten minutes' peace – to make an important phone call, do something on the computer, tidy up the house – or simply put my feet up.'

Chapter 6

How to keep to the limit — the 7 Golden Rules

Kids' tricks to keep switched on

> 'I wake up really early and I creep down and play on Sims. I'll play from 7.30 for about an hour.' *11 year old girl*

> 'I say I've worked so hard today. I really deserve it.' *11 year old girl*

> 'My mum sometimes takes the keyboard away. Except my brother gets around that because he has found an on-screen keyboard. Mum doesn't know.' *10 year old boy*

> 'My mum says stop playing and go off and do something else. But I stop and go off and play on my MP3. She means go off and do some drawing.' *8 year old girl*

> 'I take my Game Boy and hide in a cupboard and play it. I lock the door with a ruler so she doesn't know I'm there.' *9 year old girl*

> 'I just wind up my mum, "please, please, please".' *9 year old girl*

Of course, children will always try and find ways of getting what they want, but we believe these tried and tested rules will get you on the right track.

1. Control

Observation:

With most games it's OK for children to play with them when and where they want. But TV and computers aren't like any other game. They need to be controlled and so should be treated very differently from anything else in the toy cupboard.

123

Golden Rule 1: Parents stay in control of TV and computers

It's important that you try and keep your child asking permission to switch on the TV or computer for as long as possible, preferably up to the age of 12. Once they're out of the habit it's hard to reinstate the rule.

If your child has to ask permission, they are more likely to recognise and value media time as different from any other time. It will also make the job of controlling your child's media consumption a lot easier for you.

> 'I noticed the TV being turned on at funny times of the day. So I got them into the habit of asking me before they switched it on.'
> *Sarah, non-working mum*

> 'They still ask to turn it on. I've just kept them in the habit'.
> *Clarissa, a Tight Controller mum*

It's important also that you have a set of ground rules for using the TV and computer, and that your child is fully aware of what they are.

> 'Goal setting is massively important. A lot of people don't know how to do it. I think a lot of children are the products of a society where it is the children who tell the parents what to do.' *Teacher of 2 to 5 year olds*

> 'Children need boundaries because they don't know what's good for them. Adults need to take that responsibility and not let children have it all their own way.' *Su, Head Teacher*

It's easier if you establish ground rules right from the start. So, before you buy your child a new computer or computer game, sit down with them and decide what the rules are.

'I've got a 15 year old – he got really obsessed by it. If you called him for meals he wouldn't come. I'm really careful for my 10 year old. I'm determined not to let it happen again. We sit down and agree what she can play. "You can play it for this long a day", I say, and no more.'

Julia, mum who's doing things differently with her second child

We came across a lot of parents who had devised different time controls for their kids.

'Jack has an evening once a week when he can have an hour on the computer games. Then Sophie has an hour another day.'

Katie, mum of four children aged 6 to 13 – but still very much in control

2. Short time units

Observation:

The longer you leave a child in front of the screen, the more difficult it becomes to drag him or her away.

Many children's television programmes are half an hour long which is plenty of time for a child to chill out or relax, before going off to do something else. Likewise, half an hour on the computer is plenty of time to complete a game, or try and move up to the next level. You also shouldn't stay too long in one position because it's better for the body if you move around at regular intervals.

Golden Rule 2: When it comes to media time – think in half hour units of time

" 'Half an hour is a reasonable amount of time to relax. It's long enough to recharge the batteries, but not so long that you get totally absorbed.'
Emma, nanny of two boys and a girl

" 'Most programmes are roughly half an hour long. It's a good length of time for a child'. *Susan, carer who looks after two families*

" 'If you've been sitting for two hours in the same position, it's really hard to think about what you're going to do next. It takes about 5 to 10 minutes to get your brain going again. The brain shuts off.'
Jenny, carer who looks after three kids and a baby

" 'I have an egg timer. It was for my piano practising, but now I use it for my computer. If I just have half an hour on the computer, then I can pause a game, go downstairs, then I come back for another half hour later, and then I know I've had an hour.' *10 year old boy*

3. Screens in the bedroom

'TV's in bedrooms, I think they're really bad.'
11 year old girl

Night-time goings on ...

"'I'm naughty and take my mobile to bed. I play with it until the batteries run out.' *8 year old girl*

"'I play my Game Boy in bed. I do it secretly under my covers. It comes up with a little light. You can get these plug in lights.' *9 year old girl*

"'I take my portable DVD to bed. I watch Friends in bed. I do it between 9 and 10.' *8 year old girl*

"'Some Game Boys are quite dark so I had to get a plug in light.' *9 year old girl*

"'I watch it late when I'm not supposed to. I turn the volume down. It makes me get to sleep easier because I'm tired. I watch too much.' *12 year old boy*

"'It depends if there's a good film on. I just turn it off when I feel like it. Like one in the morning!' *11 year old boy*.

Observation:

TVs in the bedroom was one of the most emotive areas touched on in our research. For some families it has become part of a way of life. For other parents TV in a child's bedroom is a definite 'no'.

Around 80 per cent of children aged 11 to 15 have a TV in their bedroom, although most parents don't think it's a good idea.[1]

Once you allow the TV in your child's bedroom you risk letting go of some of your control. Ideally, there should be areas of the home which are 'TV free' zones. Children's bedrooms are one such area. Children need somewhere to retreat to where they can enjoy some peace and quiet.

And, once the TV is introduced into the bedroom the bedtime story risks being dropped altogether. We were surprised at how many homes are losing bedtime stories to the TV. In one group discussion we had, a mother described how she always reads to her children before bed. The eyes of the other mums literally popped out.

Golden Rule 3: Don't allow televisions in bedrooms of under 12 year olds

Ideally, the TV should be in communal areas where you can keep an eye on who's watching what, and where it can be enjoyed by the whole family together.

A lot of televisions find their way into kids' bedrooms because of TV games consoles, such as the PlayStation. Try and resist putting the PlayStation in your child's bedroom, but if you do, there's a simple answer – don't aerial up the TV facility. This will ensure the TV is just being used as a games console screen and nothing else. And don't be afraid of confiscating any portable screens if they're being used after lights out.

And, if the TV is already working in your kid's bedroom and you can't take it out, make sure you monitor its usage closely. Try also to ensure that you watch any family programmes together as a family, rather than individually in your separate spaces.

'You abdicate control. They can watch into the small hours. It becomes parents in the dark.' *Kate, at-home mum with two boys*

'It's their private space. If you introduce the TV or computer there, you'll never see them again.' *Cheryl, part-time mum with son and daughter*

'You're setting yourself up with a problem. Our kids don't have a TV in their bedroom – TV is only in the sitting room or playroom. It's a social spot.' *Sophie, part-time mum with two girls*

'They shouldn't have a television in their bedroom. Full stop. It stops communications altogether. It stimulates the brain and you're there to relax and sleep.' *June, grandmum who regularly looks after three grandchildren*

4. Meal times

Observation:

Again, this was a very emotive area amongst the parents we interviewed. In many families having the television on during meal times has become the normal way of doing things. Other families try to ensure that at least some meals are telly free.

The TV at meal times kills conversation and distracts children from eating. Meal times are special family times. It's often the only time when the family is all together and can catch up on the day's events. Children develop their conversational skills while chatting over their tea. They also learn to listen and take an interest in others and, crucially, develop a sense of being part of a family unit.

Golden Rule 4: Watching the TV during meal times should be a treat – not the norm

Try and make meals a family event. Even if you're not eating at the same time, sit down with your children and have a cup of tea. Use it as catch up time and don't let the TV invade family moments.

'If they're glued to the telly, they're not concentrating on what they're eating.' *Nick, dad who tries to switch off during meal times*

'So many issues are brought to the table. They can tell you they've had an awful day, and somehow because you've shared it, it's better. With wall to wall telly it's difficult to have a conversation.'
Di, grandmum who has grandchildren after school

'They can have breakfast in front of the TV, but not dinner. I cook one meal only, and we sit down as a family.' *Tracey, mum who switches off for dinner*

'If someone has worked really hard on the meal, you want to appreciate it, not just gulp it down.' *11 year old girl*

'When you come to lunch you can find out what you've all been doing.' *12 year old girl*

5. Early mornings

Observation:

Starting the day in front of the TV or computer screen can get it off to a bad start. If children are watching TV or playing on the computer first thing in the morning, it's often harder to get them on to other activities. And on schools days it can be particularly distracting when you are trying to get them out of the house.

Parents we interviewed found that once they had allowed early morning TV or computer time, children were getting up earlier and earlier. It became a real incentive for kids to get up early so everyone was losing precious sleep time. Parents also pointed out the problem of not being able to supervise what their children watch or play very early in the morning. For example, young kids end up watching news bulletins that can be disturbing.

And finally, they mentioned the issue of bad behaviour. A lot of parents found that long bouts of early morning television left children in particularly bad moods – either over agitated or too soporific.

Just five more minutes, pleeese!

Golden Rule 5: Limit TV or computer time early in the morning – and avoid if possible

It's understandable that some parents – particularly those with toddlers and young children – may want to stick to some early morning TV. If kids get up early, the TV often gives parents some much needed extra time in bed.

If so, it's not a problem. Just make sure you limit it and put in some controls. For instance, you might decide no TV before a certain hour; a very limited amount before breakfast and/or your child can only watch certain channels or videos.

It's particularly important that your child comes and asks your permission first so you can keep an eye on the time. If it's too early, send them back to bed again. One mum we spoke to kept the remote control by her bedside so she knew her child couldn't watch any TV unless he came and asked her.

If your child is going to school you need to be very strict with the limit – ideally no TV in the morning, but certainly no more than 20 minutes. Interestingly, from our research we found a lot of parents use early morning TV tactically – to get kids dressed, or even out of bed. So, if your kids are into early morning viewing, try and get something positive out of it.

'My children wake up early, so we do use the TV as an early morning babysitter. But we pretend it doesn't work until 6am.'
Karen, with boys who were waking up at 5am to watch TV

'I say to my youngest that he has to be dressed and have had breakfast before he can watch it.' *Jennie, mum who uses TV as an incentive*

'They go for half an hour before school on the PlayStation. That's one way of getting them dressed in the mornings. It works well.'
Kim, mum who uses TV as an incentive

How to keep to the limit – the 7 Golden Rules

131

6. Bedtime

Observation:

A big concern amongst teachers – as well as parents – is that children are often exhausted and tired at school. One of the main reasons is that bedtime isn't what it used to be. Instead of quiet bedtime stories, kids are enjoying computer games or exciting videos just before going to bed. Screen activity before bedtime stimulates the brain and makes it more difficult for a child to go to sleep.

And then there are too many distractions in the bedroom. So, after bedtime children are still playing on the computer, watching videos and TV – and even emailing and texting friends. No wonder our kids are all exhausted.

Golden Rule 6: Don't allow any screen activity in the run up to – or after – bedtime

If need be, ban mobile phones from the bedroom after lights out, and unplug any media equipment. Make time for a calm period immediately before putting your children to bed.

Try not to lurch from the screen to bed. Children need time to unwind. The best way of doing this is reading a bedtime story. It offers a moment of calm and the chance to have a final catch up with mum or dad.

7. Wallpaper viewing

Observation:

TV isn't like music which you can easily have on in the background while doing other things. It dominates a room and can be extremely distracting. But in many homes the TV is put on first thing in the morning and stays on until last thing at night. Children get used to it and find it hard to imagine being without it.

If the television is constantly on it becomes difficult for everyone to focus on other things. It also becomes hard for a family to communicate properly with each other.

Golden Rule 7: Create periods of time without the computer or television

Clearly differentiate between television and non-television time. When it's not television time switch it off. Don't let your child, for instance, do homework in front of the TV.

133

A good way of doing this is to introduce the concept of TV planning. Encourage your child to plan their TV viewing so that they know what they're going to watch before they turn it on (*see page 166*). Once the programme is finished, the TV should be switched off.

'I try and make him watch specific things. He must have a reason for watching.' *Joanna, mum with 9 and 12 year old*

'I cut down my daughter's time in front of the TV, simply by getting her to plan her watching. At the beginning of the week she looks at the listings and tells me what she wants to watch. We then agree her week's viewing. She's actually started to enjoy picking the programmes and has fun flicking through the different TV guides to see what's on. She also enjoys the programmes more because she looks forward to them.'
Robert, dad, with one daughter aged 11

The position of screens in your home can also be important. As one mum said to us, *'It's all about where you put the screens. That's the number one consideration.'* Try and make sure that the TV doesn't totally dominate the main living area so that when it's on, it's difficult to get away from.

Louise says:

'I've found that the simplest things can make a difference. We used to have all the children's videos stacked up by the TV in the sitting room. They were on full display and so when the girls came into the room it was the first thing they saw. Just seeing them made them want to watch them. They're now hidden away, so it's not the first thing the girls think of as they walk into the room.'

Similarly, we came across parents who deliberately make sure computer games and play stations aren't too accessible. If a bit of effort is required to set things up, it can act as a disincentive – in the same way that toys at the back of the cupboard are generally the ones they play with the less.

'I try and make it difficult to get on the PlayStation. The screen is always unplugged and the handset bit of it is kept in a drawer. It doesn't stop them playing on it, but it makes them think a bit more about whether they really want to or not.'

Jane, at-home mum, trying to make access to the screen difficult

Another important point is not to have too many TV screens. Children with their own TV screen spend on average 37 minutes more watching TV each day than children without their own screen.[45]

Top 5 tips on where to put screens in the home

- Limit the number of screens – don't give each child a PlayStation, for instance

- Don't let the TV totally dominate your main living area

- Keep the TV out of kids' bedrooms

- Check there is screen-free space in the home

- Screens with internet access should be placed where you can keep an eye on them.

Problems and solutions — controlling time

Switching off

'It's all very well people saying you just have to switch it off but there's no easy way of doing it. I dread the moment so I end up delaying it as much as I can. And then there's always that confrontation – "you're the worst mum in the world," or some abuse like that. There must be a better way of doing it.'

 Tips: A few parents we spoke to – most of them dads – couldn't see what the fuss was about. 'It's easy', they said, 'you just switch it off. Don't worry about the grief, they soon forget about it.'

To a certain extent, they're right. But for most of us – particularly anyone faced with the problem every day – a 'smooth' switch off is important. If handled well, switching off shouldn't result in tantrums or be a moment we all dread as parents.

Here are a few simple tricks which might help:

• Keep your child asking permission to switch on for as long as possible.

• Agree *before* your child switches on how long they're going to be in front of the screen. You may decide to put a time limit on it, or to switch it off after a specific programme.

Watch out for computer games, though. It's sometimes difficult to set a clear cut off point because there's always another level of a game to achieve. Often a time limit is the best option. Let your child, however, wrap up a computer game in a way which makes them feel good about what they've done. You may need to allow them, for instance, to save where they are so they can go back to it later.

• Get your child to keep a check on the time. A good way of doing this is to put a clock, or timer, right next to the television or computer.

• Give them a warning before switching off – for example, 'just five more minutes'.

- Try to make the 'switching off' their responsibility. If they have to switch off the button, they often feel much better about it.

- Stick to what you've agreed – say no to, 'just five more minutes pleeese!' This is where you may need to be resilient. Take a deep breath and wait for the moment of confrontation to pass.

- Be sympathetic with your child during the 'post screen moment'. They'll probably experience a period of inertia and frustration and take it out on you.

- Get them to focus on what's next – the screen alternatives. Often a good way of doing this is to change their environment. Get them into another room, or go outside.

I'm suffering from post-screen inertia – the cold turkey moment

- Don't be afraid of letting them get bored. Children are often at their most creative when they're bored and looking for things to do.

Top tips from parents and carers

'I always get anger confrontation. You've got to stick with it and then after about five minutes it's fine.'
Felicity, mum with a strong-minded boy.

'He's very angry when I say "right, turn the TV off". Very, very cross. It takes him about 5 minutes to calm down.' *Rosie, mum who dreads the switch off*

'We've made a game of turning the TV off. My two girls take it in turns and when we can't remember whose turn it is, they race to turn off the button.'
Loulou, mum with two girls aged 2 and 4

'I'll try and get them to focus on what they're going to do next.'
Jo, carer of three families

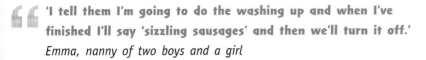

'I tell them I'm going to do the washing up and when I've finished I'll say 'sizzling sausages' and then we'll turn it off.' *Emma, nanny of two boys and a girl*

'The important thing is to have a definite routine for turning it off.' *Susan, mum with two toddlers*

'The easiest thing is to go outside and away from that room' *Julie, nanny of three kids*

'Agree a time as they sit down. It creates the right expectations and also makes them part of the process.' *Liz, mum of two girls and a boy*

'There's always a five minute period when it's "Oh, mum ...!" They don't quite know what to do. But if you let them fester long enough, they come up with an alternative. You need grit to get through that resistance period.' *Sarah-Jane, mum of two boys*

'It's saying "no" when you mean it. Parents make it hard for themselves if they say 'no' and don't mean it.' *June, grandmum with three grandchildren*

Top tips from kids to parents!

'Suggest rather than being too bossy. If things aren't allowed the child rebels. Do things gently, and suggest things.' *12 year old girl*

'Say: "you've got five more minutes, and if you don't come off, no TV tomorrow".' *12 year old girl*

'You need to reward them with pocket money.' *11 year old girl*

'Put a timetable up on the wall.' *11 year old girl*

'You have to trust your child!' *12 year old girl*

'If they've had their TV time for the day, record it so they can watch it tomorrow.' *11 year old girl*

'Don't give in, it shows you're weak.' *12 year old girl*

'Make sure they don't go back on and ban them from it if they do.'
10 year old boy

'Don't shout too much. Say, "it's my turn". Teach them what they can do instead.' *8 year old boy*

'Say, "your next door neighbour is outside, why don't you go and play?"'
8 year old boy

'Pull the plug out.' *12 year old boy*

'Get a little man on the screen who bleeps when you need to get off. And then if you don't it explodes everything.' *11 year old boy*

'Stand there and watch them turn it off.' *11 year old girl*

How kids get round 'the switch off'

'My computer has this button on the remote that changes it on to TV. She says, "Get off the Sims now and watch some TV", but I keep the Sims there, and when she's out of the room I switch.' *11 year old girl*

'I say it's almost the end of the programme, when it's just started, and then just five more minutes, until the end.' *12 year old boy*

'Mum says "better get your homework done". I say "in a minute". She comes back, says "get your homework done". I say, "in a minute". It goes on like that for about 2 hours.' *8 year old girl*

'I just keep on going, please can I go on the computer, every five minutes, until she gives up.' *9 year old boy*

'I quickly set up another match.'
11 year old boy

'I just say I'm finishing off the level.'
11 year old boy

Just five more minutes, pleeese!

Juggling kids of different ages and sex

'I've got children with very different timetables and needs. So, one child gets home from school at 3.30pm and flops down in front of the TV. Just when it's time for her to get up and do something else, my son comes home and wants some telly. So the TV ends up being on the whole time with everyone watching it.'

 Tips:

- Personalize media time so there isn't the assumption that when the TV is on it's there for everyone to watch. Create the feeling that each child has his or her special time in front of the TV – sometimes with other members of the family, sometimes on their own.

- When the time's up for one child to stop watching TV, you may need to draw them away from the screen by enticing them into another room – or into another corner of the room – to do a specific activity. It's good to have something in mind to fill the void: homework, a play activity or simply helping you prepare tea in the kitchen.

- Try and make sure that the TV doesn't dominate the main family room so that it's impossible to do anything else in the room when it's on. Even in a small room you can arrange things to create a more focused TV area and a non-TV area.

Stopping kids squabbling

'The TV and PlayStation are a constant source of friction between my kids. They're constantly arguing about who can play this or watch that.'

 Tips:

- Try and establish a sense of 'screen sharing'. Don't solve the problem of kids fighting over TV programmes or computer games by getting everyone their own screen. It's good for children to share. Get them to agree between themselves, and with you, who's going to use what when. This will also help them think carefully about how to allocate their own media time.

- One mum told us how she had introduced the idea of sharing the screen according to the days of the week. As a result her two children have the use of the PlayStation on alternate days.

- In another home we found the PlayStation was rotated around the home so every two months it would move to the next child's room.

Louise says:

'I sometimes try and turn any squabbling to my advantage. The children normally have a video after their bath and often can't agree on what it should be. I give them an incentive. The first one out of the bath can choose the video. It's normally Alice who jumps out first because she cares most about what they watch. Ophelia, on the other hand, loves water and so makes the most of the extra time in the bath.'

Coping with peer pressure

'I find it difficult to know when to say "no". Mark will come home and say that so and so has got this new computer game and he wants one too. Then if I don't let him watch certain TV programmes, he'll complain that he feels left out because everyone else is allowed to.'

 Tips:

- Try and get your child used to the concept of not having everything. Just because a friend has the latest computer game doesn't automatically mean that they should get it too.

- Do the time test. If after a certain period your child is still wanting something, you can start taking the request more seriously. Never give in straightaway. Peer pressure is all about buying the talk of the town. Before you know it things have moved on and another fad has appeared.

- Point out that it's good that different homes have different things. You don't always have to replicate what friends have got, and it's fun to enjoy games in different environments.

- Get your child to buy computer games out of their own pocket money. If they've had to save up for something, they're likely to value it more.

- And don't be afraid to chat with other parents. Check out whether what your child's saying is totally accurate. You may find, for instance, that it's not your son's friend who has the computer game, but his older brother. It's also good to share your experiences with other mums and dads.

Sport on TV

'I've got a sports mad husband who at any opportunity will be watching some sporting event on Sky. It's difficult with the kids. They see their dad sitting there and naturally want to join him. And what makes it worse is that often the big games are on in the evening so the kids end up going to bed later than they should do.'

Tips:

- Get your partner or husband to be supportive of what you're doing – it's essential that you work as a team.

- Set firm football rules and limits. So, for instance, during the week you might decide your child can only watch matches if their home team is playing. Or, at weekends you might allow them to watch the first and last twenty minutes of a game – making sure you record the whole thing so any goals missed can be replayed.

- To stop the problem of late night sports watching, you might allow your children to watch the first half of any match, and record the second half to see the following day.

- Consider using the radio to get your children away from the screen. We spoke to one mum who allows her son to watch the first half of a football match in front of the TV. He then has to turn it off for the second half, but can listen to it on the radio. So, often he'll play carpet football as he's still following the match on the radio.

 'If there's an important football match they want to watch, say, "no TV until the football", so that they keep their TV time for it'.' *12 year old girl*

Managing play dates

'My son will really look forward to a friend coming round to tea and then all they end up doing is sitting in front of the telly or playing on the computer. It seems such a waste when he can do that on his own.'

 Tips:

- Make sure that when friends come round they start off with some 'screen free' time. They can always move on to the screen once they've had some time playing together.

- Try and encourage media activity which is social. For instance, encourage two player games rather than having one child playing on the computer and the other just looking on.

Holidays

'My kids are keen to take their PlayStation on holiday with us. Is this a good idea?'

 Tips:

- Ideally, try and resist your children taking TV consoles, such as PlayStations, on holiday. Holidays are a great opportunity to broaden children's horizons so try and get them to leave screen distractions at home. It's good to have some time without them.

- If you want your child to break any bad media habits, holidays are also a good time to do it. If you leave the PlayStation at home, it'll give them a clean break and make it easier to start afresh back home.

- On the other hand, mobile consoles can be useful during long journeys. But beware. Once the travelling is done, try and get your child to pack it away so that they get a break.

- We found that several parents had specific rules for holiday screen activity. Some parents, for instance, say no TV before an outside activity, and others restrict when and for how long the TV or computer can be turned on.

" **'I have a rule in the holidays. They can't watch TV in the mornings. I noticed when they did it put them in a foul mood, so I stopped it.'**
Corella, at-home mum with three boys

Portable games

'My son wants to take his Game Boy everywhere – should I let him?'

 Tips:

- It's very important that the mobility of mobile games doesn't mean that your child never gets away from them.

- As a rule of thumb, we suggest that kids are allowed to use mobile games away from the home if they're having to wait around or be patient. For instance, if a sibling is having a swimming lesson then let your other child play on their mobile game. But don't let mobile games intrude on other activities, or social occasions.

145

- Look out for the new generation of mobile games – the Sony PSP (PlayStation Portable) and Nintendo DS. With the bigger screens these handheld consoles offer a game experience that is far closer to TV than the original Game Boys. This means that they will become more compulsive and less of a second best. So, there will be more of a need to keep a check on how your child is using them.

- Remember that playing on a portable game, be it a mobile phone game, or a handheld console, counts as screen time. Just because your child is playing while you are out and about, doesn't mean that you shouldn't keep an eye on how long they are playing. It should be counted as screen time and your child should understand that it is included in his or her daily quota.

Screen media used for incentives or rewards

'Can I use the TV and computer as a reward for doing things?'

 Tips:

There are some people who believe that using rewards isn't a good idea because it sends out the wrong messages to your child.

From our research we found that parents were successfully using the TV and computer as rewards or incentives for doing things – for instance, getting dressed and having breakfast in the morning, or finishing homework in the evening. So, yes, use them as a reward if it helps you. But don't do it the whole time. Don't let yourself become too dependent on the TV or computer for getting things done.

 'I use the TV and computer for rewards – in the same way as sweets or other treats. It works for us. It makes the kids value their screen time because it's not automatic, they've earned it.' *Jacky, part-time working mum with two kids*

The dangers of MSN

'Should I let my child use MSN? I've heard how some kids become totally obsessed by it.'

 Tips:

MSN (or Microsoft Network) has become the standard online meeting place for kids aged 10 and upwards. It allows them to access an instant messaging network, which is far more spontaneous than email. Kids define who they want to talk to through the address book scheme. These are lists of contacts that individuals can set up through a mutual request system, and most of the kids we spoke to had books with well over 50 contacts. Kids also have fun blocking people from their address books, for instance, a friend who has become a bit of a pain, or simply a friend of a friend who can't be trusted.

 'I've got about 80 people in my address book. After school at 6-ish I'll find at least 10 of them to talk to.' 11 year old girl

 'You can drop people from your address book. I did that with this person who lied to us. He said he had a brain tumour. It was scary.' 12 year old girl

 'If you don't want to talk to someone you can block them.' 11 year old girl

MSN is a wonderful vehicle for building friendships and keeping in contact with old friends. It is particularly great for kids who live some distance from their school. For example, one single mum described how she and her son lived in a remote village. Driving her son around to visit his chums is a problem for her but with MSN he feels in touch, and doesn't feel as isolated as before.

What's more, MSN prepares kids for the adult world where corporate instant messaging systems are becoming the norm.

 'Increasingly we use instant messaging – it means I can see who is about – and more importantly I can check out whether they are in the mood to talk.'
Andrew, IBM Consultant

But watch out – it can become an obsession

We believe that MSN is a great networking tool for kids, but it does need to be monitored carefully. In some homes it has become an enormous drain on kids' time, and mums described how they had to keep it under control. One mum said her son would happily spend 6 hours on MSN if she didn't limit it, and we spoke to many girls who seemed to be online all evening. It is easy for it to become an obsession – kids like to feel part of the crowd – and if you know your friends are chatting online it's hard not to join them.

> 'When my friends say, "you weren't there last night", I feel I let them down, I feel I should be there, even when I want a break.' *11 year old girl*

MSN can also be a big homework distraction. There is a function that allows you to reduce the MSN screen from full screen to pop-up size. Many of the girls we spoke to described keeping in touch with friends while they were doing their homework. Parents are often fooled into thinking they are working hard – but in fact they are constantly being diverted by the chatter.

Kids' views on MSN

> 'MSN is what I spend most time on.' *11 year old girl*

> 'I found it really difficult with everybody just saying "hello, hello". Not much else.' *11 year old girl*

> 'I play games like naughts and crosses. It passes the time.'
> *12 year old girl*

> 'We use webcam so you can see your friends. If you have a bad hair day, you don't have to. And we have audios. We record videos and send them to our friends.' *12 year old girl*

> 'On the last few days we've done a tree house, and I haven't been on MSN once. And I've achieved so much.'
> *An 11 year old girl who feels pleased that she hasn't wasted too much time on MSN over the last few days*

So, with MSN what would we suggest?

Firstly, we would encourage you to introduce kids of ten or over to MSN. If they are interested help them set up their own network of friends. Then keep a close eye on how they use it. If they simply use it to have a quick catch up from time to time, there's no need to impose restrictions. However, if you sense that MSN is beginning to consume too much time, then be quick to take action. Decide on what limits feel right for you and your kid – and consider it as a form of screen entertainment that needs to be embraced within the 2-hour daily limit.

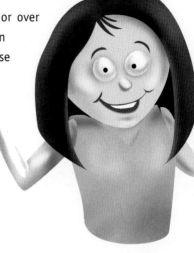

Step 1 – Summary

- The first step in The Media Diet is about setting limits – limiting the time that your child is entertained in front of the TV or computer screen.

- The Media Diet recommends '2 hours' of screen entertainment time as the upper limit for a daily average across the year.

- The '2 hour' limit should be used as a rule of thumb. The important thing is that you have a figure to aim for, and become conscious of how much time your child is spending in front of the screen.

- The diet gives you advice on planning your own family schedule, a set of 7 Golden Rules and some helpful tips.

From junk programming to healthy media – making children's screen time quality time

STEP 2 – FROM JUNK PROGRAMMING TO HEALTHY MEDIA

... MAKING CHILDREN'S SCREEN TIME QUALITY TIME

- how to become a media-savvy parent

- how to raise a media-savvy child

- problems and solutions

How to become a media-savvy parent

To make your child's media time quality time, you need to become a media savvy parent.

'What's that?' you're probably asking yourselves. It's simple. You need to be able to tell whether a TV or computer programme is good or bad for your child.

But here's where it's slightly more tricky. You don't just look at the programme and decide whether you like the look of it or not. A media-savvy parent also observes his or her child to see how they're responding to what they see on the screen.

It's the response from the child – not just the programme content – which is the thing to look out for. A positive response means quality media time. No child is the same and that's why it's important that you develop your own media antennae. What's good for one child, might be bad for another. One child might mimic the actions of Power Rangers, while another one won't. Some children may pick up the bad language of The Simpsons, while others just sit back and enjoy a good belly laugh.

Louise says:

'I had a good example of this the other day. At the moment Ophelia (3 years old) adores the video Nemo. She loves all the different fish, and particularly Bruce, the shark. What she likes best about Bruce is his wide, toothy grin. Ophelia watched Nemo with a friend, Anna, who's roughly the same age and very similar in character. But Anna would have none of it. To her, Bruce was a monster and the whole underwater world was just too spooky.

So, Snow White was chosen instead. Now it was Ophelia's turn to have a fit. The wicked Queen was too frightening and she hid her head in the corner of the sofa. Anna meanwhile was as cool as a cucumber.'

153

The Media Diet is not prescriptive. It doesn't recommend some content being good for children and some being bad. It will help you make your own judgements about how television and computer programmes affect your child. And to help you do this, we're going to share with you some of the tricks of the media trade. If you're going to be media savvy, you need to know how the media works and why.

Tricks of the media trade

As media professionals we both have extensive experience of trying to manipulate the media to influence people's thoughts and lives. The Media Diet taps into the lessons we've learnt over the years.

A simple technique in advertising, for instance, is to get people to think of brands as people. So, if you're trying to promote a car you might give it the personality and characteristics of a reliable friend, or a fast sexy lady.

UNDERSTANDING HOW YOUR CHILD RESPONDS

Imagine the TV turning into a monster, and watch out for the response ...

... now imagine the TV turning into a clown juggling for your child, with long arms that are perfect for tickling.

QUALITY RESPONSE = QUALITY TIME

It's the response that determines the quality of screen time

As parents we should look at the television and computer in the same way – as a person. Just as advertisers look out for the response that their brands have on consumers, we should look more closely at how our children respond to different aspects of the screen.

So, looking at how your child responds to an individual programme is *as important* as keeping in touch with programme content. Make sure you don't just switch on the TV or computer and walk away. Take a little time out to sit down with them and simply observe how they respond.

How is your child affected by media content?

Checking out the response

Once you start thinking of the television or computer as a person, you naturally start asking yourself some questions.

- Do I like this person and am I happy for him to be my child's playmate?

- Do I like the influence he has on my child or the mood he leaves them in?

- Is my child learning useful things from him, or does he leave them with no motivation or energy to do anything?

We have identified 7 Responses which are fundamental to how children relate to a TV or computer programme. They are:

1. **Learning** – what learning does my child take out of the programme?

2. **Motivation** – what does the programme motivate my child to do?

3. **Energy** – how does the programme influence my child's energy levels?

4. **Language** – what language does my child adopt as a result of the programme?

5. **Role models** – what role models does the programme give my child?

6. **Emotions** – how does the programme influence the mood of my child?

7. **Relationships** – does the programme encourage my child to be social, and if so, in what way?

It is important that as parents we understand the character of these different responses, so that we can appraise the quality of a programme.

The 7 Responses offer parents a framework for questioning. A parent can focus on each area and consider – is my child responding to a specific TV programme or computer game in a positive or negative way? This questioning will automatically help parents decide whether a programme should, or shouldn't, be included in a child's media schedule.

THE RESPONSE CHECK

Positive responses   Negative responses

Positive		Negative
Is my child getting valuable information, e.g. educational, world issues, street news?	◄ **Learning** ►	Is my child exposed to unsuitable information, e.g. violence, sex, disturbing news?
Is my child motivated to do something positive, e.g. a new hobby, explore a new subject, help others?	◄ **Motivation** ►	Is my child left demotivated to do anything positive, e.g. play apathy, bored, no interest in life
Does it leave my child with an appropriate energy level, e.g. restored after school, calm before bed?	◄ **Energy** ►	Does it leave my child with an inappropriate energy level, e.g. lethargic after breakfast, hyper before bed?
Will my child's language improve as a result of it, e.g. new vocabulary, positive tone of voice?	◄ **Language** ►	Is it bad for the development of my child's language, e.g. limited vocabulary, bad words, aggressive tone of voice?
Does it contain positive role models, e.g. do I respect their values, outlook on life, priorities?	◄ **Role models** ►	Does it contain negative role models, e.g. people and behaviour I don't respect, violent, anti-social behaviour?
Do I like the emotional state it leaves my child in, e.g. happy, fulfilled, confident?	◄ **Emotions** ►	Am I concerned about my child's emotional state after they switch off, e.g. sad, frightened, disturbed, aggressive?
Does it encourage good relationships between siblings, and/or with friends?	◄ **Relationships** ►	Is my child turning into a loner as a result of it?

If YES...
it's a reason to
stay tuned

◄——————►

If YES...
it's a reason to
switch off

||||

BEING SENSITIVE TO YOUR CHILD'S REACTIONS

Look out for their body language while they are engaged in media – it says so much

Judge the mood of your child immediately after – e.g. how well do they play with siblings?

Get into your child's mind – e.g. what have they remembered about the programme?

Be sensitive to how a programme is anticipated – are they really looking forward to it?

Developing important parenting skills ... developing media antennae!

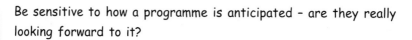

Media-savvy parents need to be sensitive to their children's reactions. Ideally, you need to look out for, and tune into, certain signs. These include:

Body language

Look carefully at your child's body language when they're in front of the screen. It can tell you so much.

Every child's body talks in a different way. Some children, for example, sit on the edge of the chair when they are captivated by a programme, while others start twisting their hair as soon as they really get into something good. As a parent you'll be in tune with your child's body language. Use this natural intuition to help you interpret whether you like the effect that a programme is having on your child.

You can often find out more about what a child is thinking or feeling if you get them to express themselves through gestures.

Teresa says:

'I often use the thumbs-up gesture when I'm doing research with children. They might tell me one thing, but I'll know what they're really thinking when I see them put their thumbs up or down. It's the conviction with which they do it that tells me exactly how much they value what they've seen.'

Mood

Judge the mood of your child immediately after they've finished a TV or computer programme. How well, for instance, do they play with their siblings?

If you're a teacher or a children's researcher you are very conscious of the way that a clip from the TV can completely transform the mood and energy of a group of children.

As parents we are very conscious of when a child becomes bad company after a particular computer game or TV programme. Look out for the mood swings in your child. Does your child become more or less responsive to you? Are they left feeling detached from the real world? Are they motivated to get on with the next thing, or does it leave them lethargic and irritable?

Thought waves

Try and tune into your child's thought waves. What have they remembered about the programme and what did they think of it?

Meal time is a good moment to catch up on what they've been viewing on TV, or doing on the computer. Kids love talking about TV and computer games. So check you're in the loop. If they sense you are interested it is amazing how quickly they will start telling you things automatically.

An important trick when digging deep into children's thoughts and reactions is to ask things in a variety of ways. You may find your first question misses the point, so have a go at asking it in a different way. Another trick when you're chatting with your children is always to move from the general to the more specific. Ask the vague questions first – like 'what did you think of that?' This vagueness allows the child to answer the question in their own terms. They will talk about what meant the most to them.

Anticipation

Be sensitive to how a programme is anticipated. Is your child really looking forward to it?

When you're researching children's reactions to a brand, you try to get a steer on how eagerly the new brand will be anticipated by children. It is the measure of anticipation that reflects how much they value it and want it to be part of their lives.

In most families there are some programmes which are anticipated with more excitement than others.

Teresa says:

'I know that in our household it's The Simpsons. The children look forward to sitting down at 6 pm to watch them. Virtually nothing will stop them.'

Louise says:

'In our home it's Noddy. If I get the timing right and the girls can watch ten minutes of Noddy on TV in the morning, then everyone's happy.'

Putting the Response Check into action

To help get you thinking about what to look out for, here are some positive and negative responses from parents to modern media.

160

Response 1 - Learning

➕ TV and computer games ... make it fun and easy to learn things ...

❝ 'Palin is great. We all sit down together as a family. Programmes like that are an amazing introduction to factual subjects that can be pretty boring – subjects like history, geography or even science.' *Simon, dad*

❝ 'Even a soap can teach you something about real life by giving you a hook to talk about things. Soaps often raise moral or social issues which you can then discuss together as a family. Like the other day EastEnders had the teenage pregnancy.' *Jackie, mum*

❝ 'All three of my grandsons are dyslexic. They just seem to excel at computer games. There're not constrained by the problems of writing. Computer games give them such a boost – they love them and they're good for them because they tap into their reason and logic.' *Sharon, grandmother*

❝ 'Some of the computer games are fantastic at teaching them things. The game Tom really enjoys at the moment has a purpose to it. There's the excitement of doing it, and often he's learnt something along the way.' *Charlie, dad*

➖ ... *Or* ... they're full of stuff I'd prefer they didn't know about

❝ 'I didn't realise it (Grand Theft Auto) was for 18 year olds until we got it home. There's stuff in there that I'd prefer he hadn't seen.' *Peter, dad*

❝ 'I definitely wouldn't want my girls playing that (Grand Theft Auto). I suppose I want to protect them from what's in there.' *Neil, dad*

Response 2 – Motivation

➕ TV and computer games ... encourage kids to do all sorts of things ...

❝ 'The dance mat games are brilliant. The children copy the dancers – at least they try to. If you buy one of those dance mats it gets them active, which is great. They're also interacting with their friends.' *Fiona, mum*

❝ 'Art Attack is fantastic. George was hooked on it. He'd watch it and then we'd spend the rest of the afternoon covered in sticky tape.' *Elsa, mum*

161

'Fantasy Football gives kids a lot to think about. They've got to think strategy, tactics and all the rest of it.' *Ray, dad*

— ... *Or* ... they leave kids feeling empty – not knowing what to do

'He has this 'shoot 'em up' game, and after half an hour on that he comes off kind of mesmerised. He's at a loose end and can't think what to do next.' *Jo, mum*

Response 3 – Energy

+ TV and computer games ... recharge the batteries after a day at school or relax them after lunch ...

'I let them watch twenty minutes of television when they come in from school and it does the job. It gives them a chance to relax and get back their energy levels.' *Christine, nanny*

'Sometimes the kids just need to flop in front of the TV and be a zombie for a while. There's so much going on that they need that time to sort themselves out. They're then ready to get up and do their homework, or anything else that needs to be done.' *Sophie, mum*

— ... *Or* ... make them totally hyper

'I had to stop him playing it before bed because it was one of those games that left him really agitated.' *Sally Anne, mum*

Response 4 – Language

+ TV and computer games ... encourage them to develop their language skills ...

'Some programmes are really good for extending vocabulary. Sesame Street is a good example. They concentrate on a letter each programme.' *Linda, mum*

'Programmes where they learn songs are good. My kids loved the Tweenies and it taught them a lot about words and speech.' *Clare, mum*

— ... *Or* ... they soak up bad language

'There's this game that's constant swearing. I know he's picked it up from there. If he swears at me I give him one on the nose.' *Carolyn, mum*

Response 5 – Role models

TV and computer games ... introduce them to good role models ...

'Blue Peter is a good role model for kids. They do lots of stuff for charities and encourage them to collect for things. It's very good at getting kids engaged and motivated.' *Lucinda, mum*

'The Bill I think is quite good because the baddy normally gets caught. I'd rather they watched that than some of the other soaps.' *Sue, mum*

... *Or* ... bad ones

'It's the music videos I don't like. They listen to this urban stuff, and then there're out there with their hoods. They think being a bully is cool.' *Kim, mum*

Response 6 – Emotions

TV and computer games ... help them become more in touch with their emotions and put them in a good mood ...

'SpongeBob SquarePants has increased their appreciation of humour. They'll sit around the table talking about what they've seen and saying why they thought it was so funny.' *Uri, mum*

'FIFA gives him an element of confidence. He's learnt so much because of the interaction with TV and the FIFA game. When he gets on the pitch, he can talk the language, and have that social interaction with his pals.' *Sara, mum*

'My middle son has got special needs. Sometimes he and my other son will go off and play a game and you can hear them laughing. If he's good at the game it makes him feel good, which is important.' *Kim, mum*

... Or ... *put them in a bad mood*

'If he loses he gets so frustrated. It's a real problem.' *Kirsty, mum*

'He's a different boy after seeing Power Rangers. Jumping all over the sofa. Impossible to control.' *Lisa, mum*

Response 7 – Relationships

TV and computer games ... help bring friends and family together ...

'The thing that provokes the biggest reaction with our granddaughter is the X Factor. She loves it and it's something we can all do together.' *Fran, grandmother*

'The Monopoly computer game. We all play it. It's brilliant because it's fun and gets us all together.' *Deborah, mum*

'Playing crazy golf. It's acting as a bond between our two children.' *Katie, mum*

'They would be isolated children without some form of screen. Children don't like to be different.' *Simon, dad*

... *Or* ... pull them apart

'We had it with Sims. She wouldn't do anything else. She'd go up to her room by herself and stay there for hours on end. She'd prefer to be there – rather than with friends.' *Clare, mum*

Now think about how your child responds to individual TV programmes and computer games. Here's a Response Check for you to fill in, or get a copy from www.mediadietforkids.com

THE RESPONSE CHECK

Positive responses ➕   Negative responses ➖

Positive responses		Negative responses
	← **Learning** →	
	← **Motivation** →	
	← **Energy** →	
	← **Language** →	
	← **Role models** →	
	← **Emotions** →	
	← **Relationships** →	

If YES...
it's a reason to
stay tuned

⟵⟶

If YES...
it's a reason to
switch off

Name of TV programme/computer game
....

165

TV planning and buying computer games

TV planning

With such a wide choice of TV channels now available, it's a good idea to plan your child's TV viewing in advance.

Getting into the routine of advanced planning gives you better control over the amount of time your child spends in front of the TV, and what they watch. It also encourages your child to start taking on their own screen responsibility. They have to be selective and make choices for themselves.

One teacher described to us how a child she knew had been encouraged to take on responsibility for his own TV viewing.

'His mum encouraged him to select his own TV programmes. Because he was given the responsibility he took it very seriously. He would choose which programmes he thought were suitable for him. And it even got to the point where if he started watching one and thought it wasn't quite right for him, he would turn the set off.' *Su, Head Teacher*

So if your child is old enough, it's important that they're involved in any planning too. This gets them to think about what they really enjoy, and appreciate more what they watch.

'Mum says before you turn on the telly, look to see what's on the telly pages. We see when the new series are. If everyone got into the habit of looking at telly pages, you wouldn't just slob out with nothing good on.' *10 year old boy*

We spoke to one dad who had made the selection process a fun activity in itself, and one mum told us how programme selection was key to how she limited her daughter's TV screen time.

'I think it's all about planned viewing. From an early age we used to discuss with Genevieve which programmes she wanted to watch. She would then watch it at the pre-arranged time until it was over. It tended to discourage TV browsing.' *Sandra, mum of daughter aged 12*

Teresa says:

'I now try and make the children plan most of their TV viewing. Before it was all slightly haphazard. I've noticed, however, not only a drop in the amount of time they spend in front of the TV, but in their whole attitude. They seem to appreciate programmes a lot more than they used to do – and they enjoy the fact that they're actually making choices.

The other day Chris was kicking a ball outside. He said he was going to save his screen time for later in the day because there was a good programme on and he wanted to watch it.'

And if programmes are on at inappropriate times, record them. It's much better that kids watch programmes at times which suit their schedule, rather than letting them disrupt the family routine. There are new digital services such as Sky⁺ and TiVo that make the job of recording so much easier. These services allow you to select programmes in advance, and the recording is done automatically for you. We spoke to an early adopter of the Sky⁺ service who had been using the service for a year and a half. He told us how the service had transformed the way he and his wife watch TV.

'It makes recording so easy. At a click of a button, I can see the schedule for the week and I just highlight all the programmes I want to watch, and they're recorded automatically. If I want a review of a programme, I just click for it. It's great for series, I only have to click on it once and then it automatically records the whole series. It's transformed how we watch TV. I'd guess that 95 per cent of what we watch is pre-recorded. It means we can watch what we want when we want.' *Adrian, early adopter of Sky⁺*

Don't be afraid of trying out new programmes, or insisting on programmes that sound worthwhile. Read the reviews of programmes coming up and see if anything sounds as though it might interest your child. TV documentaries can be a wonderful source of inspiration and a great way to learn things as a family.

Teresa says:

'I recently had a rebellion from Chris who didn't want to watch a documentary about the British Isles. 'Oh that guy Alan is so boring – he's just for 40 year olds', was his response. I persevered saying it was my turn to choose a programme. At first he turned away, but in no time he was back – totally captured by the history of the ice age!'

And remember, if you can sit down for five minutes, watch the TV with your child. The more you can keep in touch with what they're watching, and see how they're reacting, the better.

Finally, don't forget, the whole point about TV planning is that once you've watched your chosen programme, you turn the TV off. Just because the TV's on, doesn't mean you should let your child continue watching it.

Film ratings

When it comes to planning what films to watch at home (TV, video and DVD), or at the cinema, it is important for parents to be up-to-date with the subtleties of the ratings systems. For instance, do you know the differences between a PG and a 12 rated video/DVD? The PG rating tells you that the content is suitable for children aged 8 years and over, while the 12 rating tells you that the content is suitable for children aged 12 years and older. The 12A category is a cinema category that allows younger children to go to 12 rated films with an accompanying adult, but it is important to note that the material in any 12 or 12A film is not always suitable for them.

The British Board of Film Classification (see separate box opposite) classifies films in the UK, and their website (www.bbfc.co.uk) is well worth a visit. For instance, they give a short description of recent films and explanations of why they have been given a particular rating. There is also a children's section that explains how the ratings are decided, and it encourages kids to understand why ratings are important. This is important territory for you to discuss with your children. We all know that it is impossible to completely control what a young child views at home, particularly when there are older siblings about. But we believe that ratings are important, and if your kids have an appreciation of the system, and know that you believe in it, it will make it easier to monitor what they view.

WHAT IS THE BRITISH BOARD OF FILM CLASSIFICATION?

The British Board of Film Classification is an independent organisation that exists to regulate and classify the content of films shown in cinemas and released on video and DVD.

While the BBFC's classifications remain advisory with regard to cinema releases, the 1984 Video Recordings Act gave it statutory powers for the first time. Almost all UK video / DVD releases have to be examined and classified by the BBFC.

At the same time the BBFC was also made responsible for classifying the more risky computer games. These are the games that are considered by law to need classification – you can spot them because they will have a BBFC 12, 15 or 18 classification sign – rather than the voluntary PEGI or ELSPA classification sign.

The BBFC awards its classifications based on what it considers to be the appropriate age limits for the film in question - and, if deemed necessary, by requesting that the distributor makes changes to the film or game, usually in the form of cuts.

There is often a short description on the back cover of a video, DVD or game that gives a flavour of why the content was given the particular age rating.

For more information: www.bbfc.co.uk and www.bfi.org.uk

(The BBFC logo and symbols are the property of the BBFC and they are both copyright and trademark protected)

The bbfc classifications currently in use are:

Uc - This denotes video releases deemed particularly suitable for pre-school children.

U - This stands for 'Universal' and denotes that a film is suitable for everyone.

PG - This stands for 'Parental Guidance'. Although anyone can be admitted, PG certificate films contain an implicit warning that the film might contain material unsuitable for very young children.

12A – Replaced 12 at the cinema. Suitable for children of 12 and over, but children under 12 permitted if accompanied by a responsible adult.

12 – This covers videos and DVDs considered appropriate for 12 year olds and upwards. No one under 12 can buy or rent them.

15 - This denotes that the film is unsuitable for children under the age of 15, and limits cinema viewing and video / DVD purchasing and rental to people 15 years and over.

18 - This denotes that the film is unsuitable for people under the age of 18, and limits cinema viewing and video / DVD purchasing and rental to people 18 years and over.

R18 - This classification was exclusively intended for videos that could only be sold in licensed sex shops. In other words, pornography.

Top tips to TV planning

- Plan ahead using TV guides and listings
- Read the reviews carefully
- Involve your child in making the choices – keep the TV guide where they can find it
- Don't be put off by awkward timings – you can video programmes, if need be
- Try and choose a mix of programmes – don't be afraid of saying it's your turn to choose
- Be in touch with the ratings system and use it
- Switch off once the programme is finished!

Buying computer games

Once you've bought the computer or games console for your kid – for instance, the PlayStation, Xbox and GameCube – the next decision is what games to buy.

Think of computer games in terms of:

- What they get your kid to do, and ...

- What kind of world they encourage your kid to step into.

So, for instance, start distinguishing between games that are all about fast action and eye and hand coordination, and games that are designed to get your child thinking. Some games are great at making children process information and take decisions, others are good at encouraging speedy reactions.

Notice the difference also between games where kids step into a fun fantasy world, and games where they enter a world of violence and aggression. And look at how true to life the different worlds seem.

In the chart below we've created four key groups of computer games. There are lots of ways that computer games can be categorised, but when we talked to parents we found that these distinctions were the important ones.

For each group of games, we've included some points to consider if you're looking to buy a particular game. Ideally you want your child to have a healthy mix of different games. It's the overdosing on too much of the same thing that often leads to problems.

> 'Children need a variety of computer games and need to be encouraged to swap them around regularly.' *Head Teacher*

Then we've taken a separate look at educational games and software. These are games that are more about learning than entertainment, and it is territory where parents need to take the initiative. There are some fantastic programmes about, and although the kids won't be pestering you for them, they are well worth looking at.

When buying a computer game, make sure you do your research. Check the age rating and any information given out on the game, either from the manufacturer or independent reviews. A good source of advice and information can be other parents. Find out if they have views on a particular game, and even get their kids to give you a demonstration of the game in action. Computer magazines also provide game demos.

Alternatively, you can borrow games from the local library to help you decide whether or not to buy them. We came across one mum who bought her computer games from a shop where they have a return policy within 10 days if you don't like the game.

> 'I tend to buy computer games at a shop where they have a return policy within 10 days if you just don't like the game. I bought Medal of Honor the other day for my 9 year old – it just felt too violent for us. So I took it back. Simon doesn't seem to mind – he has had a go – so he can talk about it with his chums – but he isn't being exposed to all that violence all the time.' *Gillian, mum with boy aged 9 and girl aged 12*

Finally, don't forget that computer games can be downloaded from the internet and can often come as part of your computer hardware package. If this is the case, you need to check that you're happy with them. If not, you can ask the hardware provider not to load the games on to the hardware drive, but to supply them on discs which will give you more control.

The four groupings of games which we have identified are:

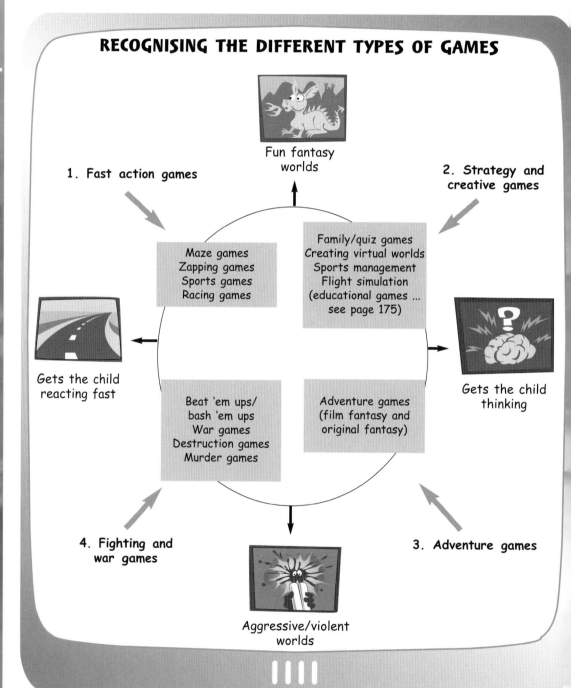

RECOGNISING THE DIFFERENT TYPES OF GAMES

Fun fantasy worlds

1. Fast action games

2. Strategy and creative games

Maze games
Zapping games
Sports games
Racing games

Family/quiz games
Creating virtual worlds
Sports management
Flight simulation
(educational games ...
see page 175)

Gets the child reacting fast

Gets the child thinking

Beat 'em ups/
bash 'em ups
War games
Destruction games
Murder games

Adventure games
(film fantasy and
original fantasy)

4. Fighting and war games

3. Adventure games

Aggressive/violent worlds

1. Fast action games

These are good for hand and eye coordination, but they can be intellectually limiting if your kid spends too long on them. This is the territory of sporting and racing games, and the fantasy the child enters can be very real to life. So, you can believe you're driving a Formula 1 racing car at the Grand Prix, or playing football in the Premier League. Examples of these types of games are FIFA, TT SuperBikes and Gran Turismo.

2. Strategy and creative games

Parents can buy these games with confidence because they're designed to get kids thinking. They include family quizzes; the creation of virtual worlds; strategic war games; sports management; flight simulation and educational games. Examples of these types of games are Sims and Roller Coaster/Zoo Tycoon.

3. Adventure games

Games of this type will often involve a voyage or mission, with tasks and obstacles along the way. The fantasy is often from a film or favourite TV programme. These games are good for decision-making skills, but as a parent you need to check you're happy with the imagery. Examples here include many classics such as Lord of the Rings, James Bond, Tomb Raider, Doom and Sonic, and The Simpsons: Hit & Run.

4. Fighting and war games

These include beat 'em ups and bash 'em ups; combatitive war games; wrestling and murder games. As in adventure games the player may be challenged to compete a number of missions – but in this territory the heart of the experience is about the fighting and destruction.

The suitability of these games for kids can be a concern for parents. Some are pure good fun, while others are OK in moderation. But many of these games are not suitable for young children and you will find they are rated 15 or 18.

It's important for parents to follow the advice of ratings and stick to their instincts – particularly when imagery and graphics become too realistic.

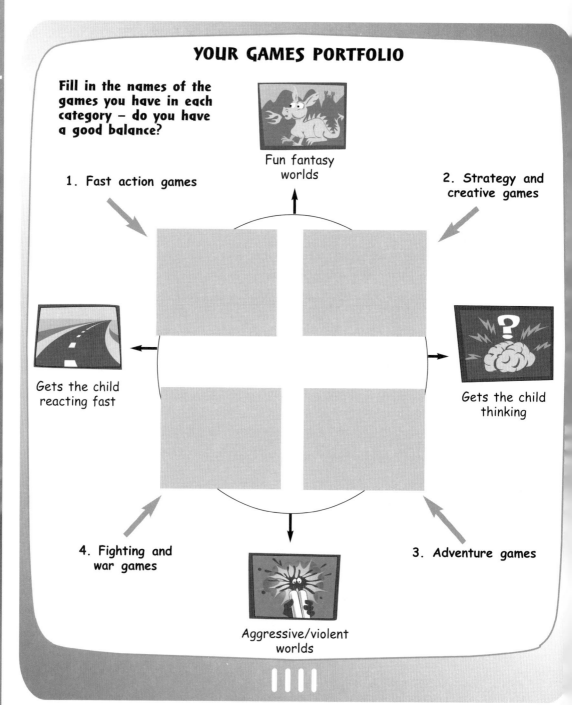

YOUR GAMES PORTFOLIO

Fill in the names of the games you have in each category – do you have a good balance?

Fun fantasy worlds

1. Fast action games

2. Strategy and creative games

Gets the child reacting fast

Gets the child thinking

4. Fighting and war games

3. Adventure games

Aggressive/violent worlds

Buying educational games and software

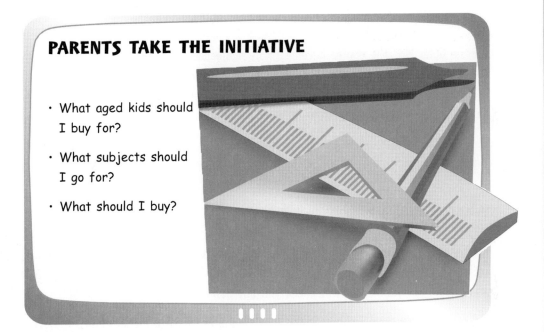

PARENTS TAKE THE INITIATIVE

- What aged kids should I buy for?

- What subjects should I go for?

- What should I buy?

What aged kids should I buy for?

Some parents start buying educational games and software for kids as young as 2 or 3 years old. There's nothing wrong with this as long as everyone understands that the computer isn't just like any other toy. It comes with certain rules.

Educational games become particularly valuable when your kids are aged between 4 and 7 years old. This is the age when they're still happy to engage in 'learning fun' and enjoy doing things encouraged by mum and dad.

Once kids reach the ages of between 7 and 12 it becomes more difficult to maintain their interest in educational material, mainly because they've discovered the likes of the PlayStation. Keep buying for this age group, however, because there's lots of good material out there.

175

What subjects should I go for?

There are lots of excellent programmes to help build literacy and numeracy skills for the under 7s.

For the older kids the choice becomes more subject-specific. For example, programmes which are designed to support schoolwork and revision. Alternatively there are creative and multi-activity programmes which have a wide age appeal, and are particularly popular with girls.

Specific programmes are also available to improve IT literacy, typing skills and language learning.

What should I buy?

The best source of advice about what to buy will come from other parents. Try and get some advice also from teachers at school. They should have a good idea about what's right for your child. But check you buy games which are fun to do at home.

It's good also to shop around. Online brochures often have a bigger choice than the High Street stores, so explore sites such as www.brainworks.co.uk. The Parents' Information Network (www.pin.org.uk) provides evaluations of educational software and websites for kids.

Once you've identified a specific educational game or piece of software, you need to decide whether it would interest and motivate your child. To help you do this, we've listed 10 key questions to ask yourself.

The 10 questions to ask

1. How could the software help my child to learn?
2. Does it look and sound appealing?
3. What is the depth and range of content?
4. Will my child find it easy to use?

5. Would my child want to use it?
6. Is there any feedback on a child's progress?
7. Would my child want to return to it time and time again?
8. Does it support learning at home, or is it obviously aimed at classroom use?
9. Does it offer support for the school curriculum?
10. What support materials are there? (e.g. are there activity packs to stimulate projects away from the screen?)

Violence in computer games

The biggest concern for most parents is the level of violence introduced into some computer games. There are a number of questions to ask yourself, in order to decide whether or not a game is too violent for your child.

1. Is the killing of people the sole purpose of the game?

If you look at the computer game Manhunt, for instance, the objective of the game is to murder people. It is about the thrill of taking life away.

There are other war games, however, where there is a specific mission – for instance, to capture a bridge or gain a territory – and people get killed along the way. The objective isn't to kill, but it becomes necessary as part of the mission. We believe that this is an important distinction.

2. Are you worried that there's no respect for human dignity in the game?

Look at how the game manipulates the player's emotions. Is death or the harming of people glorified? Are you, for example, encouraged to gloat over any killings you carry out, or any harm you cause?

'If there's blood oozing off the screen, I think that's morally wrong. It's just not necessary. That's just overdoing it.' *Danni, at-home mum*

177

3. How realistic does the violence appear?

When screen violence is portrayed in a fantasy world it's easy for a child to understand that it has nothing to do with real life. However, the distinction of reality and fantasy can become blurred as violent games become more true to life.

One of the big advances in computer games over the last decade has been the improvement of computer graphics. As computer games become more like films, it becomes all the more important for parents to take a good look at the character of a game.

We spoke to one mum who described how she felt differently about violence that existed in a fantasy world, compared to violence that occurs in a world that seems close to home. A child is in no doubt that the violence in Star Wars is fantasy, while a child playing a game in an urban world of crime and street violence may not be so sure.

'When violence is too close to home – like in today's city environment with robberies, graffiti, street killings – it feels wrong. It's different from wars in historical settings or battles in imaginary lands. Games that mimic reality feel different, they feel more disturbing and are more likely to give kids ideas.'
Ella, at home mum

4. Does the age rating, or what you have heard from other sources, warn you against the game?

We noticed that parents appear to be more cautious about film ratings than computer game ratings. It's as though parents think of game ratings like the age symbol on toys – a vague guideline that's often wrong anyway.

This relaxed attitude was confirmed when we spoke to a ratings officer. He thought that the problem lies with the word 'game', because it suggests playful territory that doesn't need to be taken too seriously.

'There is a problem with parents' attitudes to ratings. People equate games with things children play with. They don't think there is a need to be too strict. But if parents don't heed the advice of the ratings, there's nothing we can do.' *Professional ratings officer*

Children naturally put parents under pressure to buy things that are out of bounds age wise. Playing an 18, after all, has more playground credibility than playing Sonic. We found plenty of 9 year olds playing 18s.

Teresa says:

'In a world where children are exposed to so much so early on, it's often hard to appreciate the need for censoring. "Mum we've seen everything", was a remark I recently got from my 9 year old son Chris. And as Chris then went on to explain to me, it's not just the naughty ones who engage in underage gaming:

'Mum, please can we get Grand Theft Auto. Everyone has played it at school. Tom has it, and he has just won the class prize. Darren has it and says it's amazing. He has found a cheat where you do a rape.'

I asked Chris if his friends who had it, also had older brothers. Yes, they did, he said. He then went on to say it was so unfair that he didn't have one.'

We found in our research that, not surprisingly, parents have difficulty keeping things away from younger siblings, and that in a lot of households when kids reach the age of 14 – particularly if they're boys – almost anything goes.

One of the justifications parents give for this, is that children are already exposed to so many dreadful events on the news. Computer games, therefore, can often seem tame in comparison.

 'My kids say, "Why is this a 15?" I suppose it does seem tame compared to what they see on the news.' Jane, working mum

We do believe it's important for parents to be more vigilant about ratings. The ratings are there to help us, and we should use them to control the quality of our children's screen time.

5. Do you feel comfortable about the game?

Above everything else, you need to listen to your instincts. You're the best judge of what is, or isn't, good for your child. So, finally, the most important question to ask yourself is whether you're happy with the level of violence or not?

Think back to The 7-point Response Check – how will your child respond to the content of the game?

179

Will your child learn about things you would prefer they didn't know – for example, the tactics of the drug barons in a corrupt underground world? Will they want to copy bad role models – for example, aggressive skateboarders who threaten the neighbourhood with their graffiti? Will they pick up bad language that you'd prefer them not to use?

These are personal moral and family issues. Don't be tempted to dodge them just because your kids put you under pressure.

One mum described to us why she had decided not to buy a particular computer game for her son. There was an advertisement on TV showing the game. It was a wrestling game with everyone jumping on each other's heads. Her son thought it was very cool and asked her to get it. The mum knew that if she got it, her son would mimic the action. She felt that the aggressive character of the game was at odds with her own values, and just didn't want her son soaking up those visions of the world.

So, stay in tune with your own values and let them guide you when you're faced with a tricky decision.

Controlling violent computer games

If the answer is 'yes' to any of the five questions above, there are a number of options you've got if you want to control your child's use of violent computer games. It needn't just be a question of whether you buy a game or not.

Your options are:

Not to buy the computer game

The younger the child, the easier this is to do. But even with older children, try not to get pressurised to buy a game if you feel it's the wrong thing to do.

If you decide not to buy, explain clearly to your child why you've taken this decision. Show them that you've taken their request seriously and done your research.

Be prepared for your child to play the game when he or she is visiting friends. It's impossible to control them all of the time, just make sure you keep the lines of communications open with your child so you know what's going on.

Hire the game from a video shop, or borrow it from a friend

This can be a good option because it allows your child to see and experience the game, without being overexposed to it. They can then be part of the playground chatter because they've played it themselves – and that's often all that kids want.

Getting a game on loan, also gives you a chance to sit down with your child and actually show them what you don't like about the game – and explain the reasons why.

Buy it, but limit its usage

The real problems with violent computer games is kids being overexposed to them. Agree with your child before you buy the game, what the rules about playing are – how long they can play it and when. If there are younger siblings, for instance, you might decide that they can't play it when they're about.

And make sure that your child doesn't just play violent computer games. Make sure they have a healthy mixture of different types of games.

Just five more minutes, pleeese!

HOW TO TELL WHAT YOU ARE BUYING

The game in pictures
These pictures are taken from the game and give you an indication of the graphic quality. Watch out for violence that looks too real

The game in words
This gives you a brief description of the game content. It will give you a sense of what the player does and what kind of world they enter. Check you feel comfortable with this description

The format
This is how you check whether the game is for a PC or a console – PlayStation, PlayStation 2, Nintendo GameCube, Game Boy, XBox

Front cover design
Beware – we spoke to parents who had been fooled by childish cartoon designs – thinking they were buying a children's game, but in fact they were buying an 18

The age rating
This tells you the minimum age the game is suitable for, based on the content of the game (see PEGI System). Beware – we spoke to one dad who had just bought an 18 for his 11 year old son – his son had hidden the rating with his thumb

The publisher
The name of the company that publishes the game, similar to a record label

The developer
The name of the studio that created the game, similar to a movie production company label

Technical specifications
These are the minimum technical parameters that your PC or console needs in order to play the game

The descriptor
This icon lets you know the type of content in the game – violence, sex, drugs, fear, discrimination and bad language (see PEGI System)

Source: www.elspa.com and Teresa Orange Research

WHAT IS PEGI?

The Pan European Games Information (PEGI) age rating system is a new, pan-European age rating system for interactive games. It is a voluntary system that is supported by the major console manufacturers, including PlayStation, Xbox and Nintendo, as well as by publishers and developers of interactive games throughout Europe.

Started in the early Spring of 2003, PEGI replaces existing national age rating systems with a single system that is identical throughout most of Europe. In the UK it takes over from the Elspa ratings system, which you will still see on games that were launched prior to 2003.

The age rating system comprises two separate but complementary elements. The first is an age rating, similar to some existing rating systems. The PEGI age bands are 3+, 7+, 12+, 16+, 18+. The second element of the new system is a number of game descriptors. These are icons, displayed on the back of the game box, that describe the type of content to be found in the game. Depending on the type of game, there may be up to six such descriptors.

The combination of age rating and game descriptors allows parents and those purchasing games for children to ensure that the game they purchase is appropriate to the age of the intended player.

Some of the more risky games will have a compulsory BBFC rating, rather than a PEGI rating. Before any game can be rated under the voluntary system it must be established that the game is exempt from legal classification in the UK, i.e., whether it needs a BBFC certificate (see separate note on BBFC).

Game contains depictions of violence

Game depicts nudity and/or sexual behaviour or sexual references

Game refers to or depicts the use of drugs

Game may be frightening or scary for young children

Game contains depiction of, or material which may encourage, discrimination

Game contains bad language

For more information visit: www.pegi.info (the Pan European system) www.videostandards.org.uk (the agents in the UK)

(PEGI symbols are the property of ISFE – Interactive Software Federation of Europe – and are copyright and trademark protected)

If you have any views on ratings, why not share them with us on www.mediadietforkids.com

What kids say about ratings ...

" 'You have to learn about these things. They shouldn't have ratings.'
9 year old girl

" 'I watch my sister's DVDs. She's 12 and she's allowed to watch 18 ones.'
8 year old girl

" 'I've watched Die and Die Again. It's this man who is indestructible. He gets killed but he comes back again and again and again.' *8 year old girl*

" 'I play 18 games, Grand Theft.' *9 year old girl*

" 'There should be a new system where it describes the film and what it contains.' *11 year old girl*

... and what they would allow their kids to watch

When asked 'Would you let your 10 year old watch an 18?' kids replied ...

'No, too much porn.' *11 year old boy*

'No because there's normally swearing or sexual content.' *12 year old boy*

'I'd let them play the younger ones, but not 18s, because there's loads of stuff they don't know about.' *11 year old boy*

'They'll get bad ideas into their heads and think they can do exactly what's in the games.' *11 year old boy*

'I'd allow 12s but not 18s, because you get all the dodgy stuff in it, and you don't want them seeing it. Don't want them copying it.' *12 year old boy*

'I don't think children should be allowed to watch things just because it's a certain rating. They shouldn't watch horrible things all the time.' *11 year old boy*

WHEN DOES A GAME BECOME TOO VIOLENT?

- when killing becomes the sole purpose
- when human dignity is not respected
- when the game becomes too true to life
- when the age rating warns against it
- when you don't feel comfortable with it

How to raise a media-savvy child

It's no use just you being media savvy, your child needs to be media savvy too.

In the early years, when your child is still relatively young, you're the one in control. As your child grows up, however, they become more independent. You're not always going to be there to help them choose which TV programmes to watch, or which computer games to play. And you won't always be able to see how they're coping with, and reacting to, what they see on the screen.

Your child needs to take on his or her own media responsibility. They need to understand the role media plays in their lives, how to make the most of it, and the best ways of protecting themselves from some of its hazards.

If you're media savvy as a parent, you can help your child become media savvy too. The best way of doing this is to sit down with your child in front of the screen and help them understand what they need to know. It may be explaining to them that advertisements try to tempt us to buy things we don't need, or that horrific murders seen on the news don't happen every day – or simply that witches don't exist.

Learning how to distinguish reality from fantasy

Children's understanding of reality and fantasy evolves as they grow up. As parents, if we understand this evolution we can help our children when they have moments of concern or anxiety caused by the screen. Once we appreciate their understanding of what's really happening on the screen, we're in a better position to be of proper help.

Do they, for instance, believe that a certain character is real or not? How much are they aware that the behaviour and action of actors in the soaps and dramas are exaggerated for effect?

The reality versus fantasy evolution

Outlined below are the different steps in a child's 'fantasy versus reality evolution'.

As well as noting down what you as a parent should look out for, we've given some tips on how best to handle your child at each of the different stages. The most important thing is to keep on discussing TV and computer content with your child, so that you have a constant reality check.

2 to 3 year olds

Children in this age group accept fantasy for what it is. They've got no reason or inclination to question it in any way.

They understand the concept of 'make believe' and 'let's pretend'. They'll happily let the media pull them into a fantasy world, and don't have any real desire to understand whether media characters are real or not. To them, the television is a box full of things. If you lifted the lid there would simply be TV objects and people within it. They actually believe what they see.

 Useful tips:

• Let them enjoy their fantasy world during these years.

• The ideas that some things are 'pretend' and some things are 'real' can be introduced to a child – but do it gently.

• Get to know how your child reacts, so you can watch out for the moments in cartoons or videos that they're likely to find scary. Be ready to reassure them that it's 'just pretend'.

4 to 6 year olds

Kids start wanting to sort out what's real and what's not.

One teacher told us of a four year old girl who had been taken to a film premiere with her grandfather who's an actor. When they got there she asked him why he was sitting down next to him – surely he had to go off onto the screen. For this particular child, the screen was the real world.

The first thing kids of this age group do is focus on the characters which are obviously not real – the cartoon characters, or characters in fantasy dramas. It becomes very important to children to be able to distinguish between fantasy and reality – and they're proud if they're able to do so.

There's a lot of questioning at this stage and kids still turn to their parents as the final arbiter. This makes it possible for parents to extend the 'make believe' if they want to. For instance, most 6 year olds still believe in Father Christmas. The television is perceived as a magical spy glass – something which lets you see into a world beyond your home and the sitting room.

 Useful tips:

• Kids of this age seem so grown up, but beware. Don't underestimate what they might find frightening. It is often the tone or feel of a programme, rather than the content, which makes the most impression.

Teresa says:

'Isabel, when she was five, found the Beatrice Potter videos too scary, although she loved the books. The pictures and story were the same, but the tone of the music and voices on the video seemed threatening to her.'

 'My children love watching Harry Potter, but I have to turn it down when the hand comes out. It's the sound that the little ones find frightening. It's not the action. It's not always the visual.' *Alison, nanny with two children*

189

- Watch out for mimicking. At this age anything on the screen is there to be copied and becomes an inspiration for real life play.

7 to 12 year olds

By the time children reach the age of 7, they have developed their own framework for interpreting reality versus fantasy. They also understand the basic principles of the television, video or computer. However, this interpretation system isn't always as sophisticated as it might seem. In particular, children find themselves in difficulty where the reality versus fantasy distinction is blurred.

Good examples of these areas of confusion are the television soaps and virtual reality games. Here, it all seems real enough – but of course, it isn't.

Teresa says:

'I recently had an interesting glimpse into the real versus fantasy world of a nine year old, through Chris. Without me knowing, he had been listening to a 'late night love' phone-in on the radio. The next day he told me about it. His account of it went something like this:

' ... a woman called in who was having an affair with two married men. She met up with them during the day and would go back to her place to make love. She didn't care about the men's families, because she said her parents had split up so there was nothing new about having affairs.

' ... a hooker then phoned up to ask why she didn't charge the men money. Then a 17 year old rang in who said that he paid £300 for hookers every week ...'

Having told me all this, Chris then wanted to know how many of our friends were hookers. He seemed to be surprised – and disappointed – when I said I couldn't think of any. Chris couldn't distinguish between what had been dramatised for effect on the radio, and normal behaviour.'

Fantasy vs Reality distinction ... how a child's understanding progresses

2-3 year olds
Accept fantasy for what it is, no inclination to think further

4-6 year olds
Sorting out what's real vs unreal becomes an important distinction

7-12 year olds
By now kids have developed their own ways of interpreting reality vs fantasy – and understand basic principles of broadcast TV vs video vs computer

 Useful tips:

• Help your child interpret situations when the reality versus fantasy distinction becomes blurred.

• Explain to them that behaviour on reality shows is far from real and families portrayed in television soaps are not like the majority of us. So, what's happening in East Enders and Neighbours isn't necessarily going on in most homes across the country. Normal and happy family situations don't make good television.

- Keep a close eye on the use of violent games which feel too real. Either keep them out of the house, or limit their use carefully.

24-hour news

And what about the news? On the one hand, the access to 24-hour global news is great. It means that we and our children know about world affairs. But on the other hand, it can give a very distorted view of life.

When we were doing our research, one granny gave us a good example of how the news can distort a child's perception of reality. It was just after the flooding in the Cornish village of Boscastle. Her grandson had seen pictures in the news of houses being destroyed, and cars being swept away. Every time it rained, in the weeks following the disaster, he was visibly distraught. He presumed that what he had seen on the television was a normal event. He was frightened that his home would also be washed away. In the boy's mind his perception of reality, as seen on the news, had become blurred with reality itself.

As parents, it's very important that we put news into proper perspective for our children. Make sure you discuss news items with your child and explain the circumstances to them.

Here are a couple of things to consider:

News is always bad news ... and if there's sex, so much the better

Louise says:

'I always found this particularly frustrating when I was trying to promote The National Lottery. We had loads of stories about the great things happening as a result of the lottery. Was any editor interested? Of course, not.

And who can blame them? Given a choice of headlines between "Lottery winner gives money to charity and goes home to his wife" and "Lottery winner rats on girlfriend and gets convicted of fraud", I know which newspaper I would want to buy.'

" 'I know everybody's life isn't rosy, but a lot of us are happy and normal, so why don't they pick on that more, and stick that on TV.' *Kirsty, part-time working mum*

So, you just need to help your child puts things into perspective.

The world in our sitting rooms

Thanks to the technology of modern media the world suddenly seems a much smaller place. So, we can be watching recent world events on our screen – the fighting in Iraq or the Tsunami catastrophe – and it all seems so near and close to home.

Children need to know that all these events aren't happening right on their doorstep. If they go outside the front door they're not going to be mowed down by an army tank, or washed up by a gigantic wave. Make sure, therefore, you differentiate clearly between local and international news.

News saturation

The media can latch on to one particular story and stay with it for weeks and weeks. This often happens in the summer when there's not much news about. If it's a bad news story – which inevitably it is – then it can start to get depressing for children.

193

Teresa says:

'I remember the Soham murders being on the news for a very long period. It was a horrifically evil crime and the coverage of it was relentless. The children were very upset by what had happened, and eventually Isabel asked me to stop listening to the news. She couldn't take it any more.'

It's important that we're sensitive to how our children respond to the news and stay in tune with their feelings.

Wising up to the commercial screen world

Modern media offers businesses a wealth of commercial opportunities. Companies can reach their customers – and target markets – quickly and relatively cheaply.

The constant pressure of companies wanting to advertise this, or sell that, can put parents under considerable strain. Kids are deluged with information and images of exciting new products. They start wanting everything they see and pestering their parents for this and that.

 'Who can blame kids wanting more? They're bombarded with ads the whole time.' *Veena, at-home mum*

As parents we have to learn to say 'no'... and mean it. We also need to manage our children's expectations. They can't – and shouldn't – have everything they want.

One granny we spoke to explained how she tackles the 'I want' pressure. She told us that if she's going shopping with her grandchildren, she'll tell them before they set off what they're going to buy. She'll also make it clear that she's not going to get them anything. There's no point in nagging me, she'll say, because I won't change my mind. And she doesn't. And because they know she won't change her mind, they don't even ask her.

Advertising

One of the most powerful means of trying to influence children to want, or do certain things, is advertising.

Teresa says:

'Being an ex advertiser, I am very conscious of the power of advertising. I love asking kids about their favourite ads, and in no time I get a sense of which brands are spending their money most effectively. At the time of our research Diet Coke and Crazy Frog ring tones were the clear winners. I asked the kids to describe why they liked these ads so much, and it was immediately evident that these two campaigns were particularly effective ... not only were they extremely popular, but both of them were communicating an important brand message to the kids.'

'The Diet Coke tortoise. I like that one. Live life. Live it to the end. He goes everywhere with the Coke can on his back. It's healthy for you. It hasn't so much caffeine. You live longer. To the full. Even though he's really old, he's still trying to kick a football.' *8 year old girl*

'Crazy Frog ... it's Bla Bla Bla. It's very funny. It's for ring tones that you can get from the internet.' *10 year old boy*

As a parent it's useful to understand what advertisers are trying to do, the techniques they use and the likely effect it will have on your child. If you understand all that, you'll be in a good position to help your child take advertising in his or her stride.

So, here are some guidelines about what to look out for at the various stages.

2 to 3 year olds

Kids of this age enjoy recognising their favourite brands on the TV, but they have little understanding of what an advertisement is. It's good to introduce the idea of advertising as early as possible to children. All you need to say at this point is that advertisements are there to tell us about a toy, or whatever, and make us want it.

195

Advertisers targeting this age group will be trying to establish their brand name in your child's early language repertoire, for example, through sing-along songs. But most of the advertising will be targeted at the mums.

4 to 6 year olds

At the age of 4, many kids still don't realise the point of advertisements. They just think of them as mini programmes or stories. But by the age of 6 most of them understand that it's making them want this or that. Advertisements start becoming useful to kids because they use them to discover new brands, and to point out what they want.

Check your child understands what advertisements are about. Advertisers will be targeting your child directly, although they still want the advertising to appeal to you. Advertisements will be designed to fuel fantasy and excitement. Advertisers will think of clever devices that a child might take on after the ads have finished, such as funny lines or actions to mimic. This is an effective way of prolonging the power of advertising beyond the commercial break.

7 to 12 year olds

By the age of 7 kids are wised up to advertisements. They know exactly what they are about and gobble them up with interest. They enjoy adults' advertisements as much as kids' ones, and start to influence what adult brands their parents buy. The family car is a classic example.

Advertisers pitch their advertisements at kids just that little bit older than their prime target, because kids of this age group always look up to the kids above them. It's the kiss of death to talk down to these kids. Advertisers tend to use a lot of boy imagery because girls are more accepting of it. This means that ads can be very male dominated.

Mums are now out of the equation altogether. Advertisers aren't looking to appeal to them.

WHAT THE ADVERTISERS ARE DOING

2-3 years old – establishing the brand name in early vocabulary

4-6 years old – giving the brand fantasy and excitement

7-12 years old – creating a brand's aspirational credentials

 A good ad normally works at a number of different levels – performing different roles for kids of different ages

24-hours-a-day shopping

The internet is creating an environment of buying 24 hours a day which encourages kids to want to buy, buy, buy. A lot of parents talked in despair about the pressure this causes. Previously parents had the power. If you didn't want your kid to have something you didn't take them shopping, and if you did, you decided which shops to visit.

Now things have changed. The shops have come to our sitting rooms and kids are more empowered to make things happen.

Teresa says:

'I am very conscious of this at the moment. I get non-stop chat from Chris about the amazing deals he and his friends have found on the web for one computer game or another. "You can get a whole bundle of really cool PlayStation games for a fiver", he said to me the other day. The expectation was just because they were available, and cheap, we should buy them.

I'm also coming under pressure from Isabel. She's been wanting a motorised scooter for some time. I've deliberately not rushed into buying one. I wanted to wait until the time was right – and check it wasn't just a passing phase. But Isabel has taken things into her own hands. She's been to eBay and knows what scooters are available and how much they cost. She's even saved up the money. Whereas before I could divert or delay the decision, now it's more difficult.'

And then once you have decided to buy something, there can be other problems. It's easy to get conned or be the victim of fraud on the net.

So, here are some quick tips on how to deal with kids and the challenge of 24-hour shopping.

 Top Tips for dealing with 24-hour shopping

- Get used to saying 'no' and meaning it. Your child mustn't assume that you're going to buy everything.
- Encourage them to save up money themselves for things they want. This will teach them to appreciate the value of things.

- Help your child to properly check out what they're planning to buy and who they're buying from. If there are terms and conditions, read them through with your child very carefully.
- Never give your child your credit card to buy things. Once they've decided what they want and you're happy with the decision, do the transaction yourself.
- Keep your kid away from any auctions on the net. It's very easy to get carried away and spend more than you can afford.

Spam

Spam has become a big problem for anyone using the internet.

Spam is any unsolicited material you receive – a phone call, text or email. It's annoying and can be offensive. Spam can also end up costing you money because you're often encouraged to phone premium rate numbers. Spam can also contain viruses which may harm your computer.

The thing that can make spam particularly difficult for kids to cope with, is that it feels so personal. You receive messages on your personal computer or mobile phone.

It's a good idea to check with your Internet Service Provider (ISP) to see what their anti-spam policies are. You might also consider installing a filter, for instance, BT Yahoo! SpamGuard Plus.

'**I find the BT Spam filtering service really effective. My email address must have got into bad hands, because suddenly I was receiving over 100 Spam messages a week. Now I don't have to read them – the filtering system picks them up, and I just double check the list in my own time before binning them all.**' *Andrew, IBM Executive*

But the likelihood is that your child will receive Spam and so here are some tips to share with them on how to deal with it.

 Top Tips for dealing with Spam

- Be careful about who you give your email address or mobile phone number to. The more people who have your details, the more risk there is of you being sent spam.
- Never open attachments from people you don't know – they may contain viruses.
- Don't respond to Spam. It will encourage the sender to keep on contacting you because they'll know that your email address or phone number is a 'live' one.
- If you do respond, be wary. Check the identity of who you're dealing with and don't be afraid of saying 'no thank you'.

- Don't click on any links in Spam. You don't know where you might end up if you do.
- Don't forward Spam on to friends. If you do you're only passing on a problem.

Protecting your child on the internet

The internet has opened a whole new world and, not surprisingly, kids have been quick to pick up on what it has to offer. This is great, but for those of us with kids it presents a whole new parenting challenge. With the arrival of the internet has come a new responsibility to protect kids – not just when they're out on the street – but in our homes. As one mum put it:

'It used to be that one only worried about them when they were outside. Now I'm worrying about them when they're in the next door room. Surfing the web sounds harmless but when you look at some of things that go on, it makes you wonder.' *Nicola, mum aware of the dangers of the net*

A lot of the parents we spoke to were struggling with how best to manage their kids' use of the internet. On the one hand they want their children to benefit from this new phenomenon. But at the same time they're naturally worried – and the biggest worry of all is control. By allowing your kid on to the internet you're letting them loose into a world where it's difficult to keep track of where they go, whom they meet and what they do.

And if that wasn't enough, in most homes, it's the kids that know more about the technology than the parents. Research shows that children usually consider themselves more of an internet expert than their parents – 28 per cent of parents describe themselves as beginners on the internet, compared with only 7 per cent of children. No wonder a lot of us feel slightly helpless.[12]

The risks of the net

There are two main risks to kids using the internet – inappropriate content and contacts.

Because of the vast amount of information on the web it's easy for children to come across material which is unsuitable for them – pornography or material which is obscene, racist or just offensive.

The contacts children make on the net can also be inappropriate. If children meet strangers on the web – in a chat room, for instance – there's no way of knowing the true identity of whom they've come in contact with, or what their intentions are.

5 Steps to net safety

Talking to parents and experts, they identified five key actions for good internet parenting.

1. Make sure you're web savvy

You don't have to be up to date with every bit of new technology, but if you want to control your child's use of the internet it certainly helps if you know what's going on. It's essential to have some idea of what the technology is and what it can do.

You may already be very conversant with the internet. If so, that's great. But beware. Just because you know your way around, doesn't mean you have a good idea of how children use the net and what they can get up to.

A good starting point, therefore, is to sit down with your child and ask them to show you how they use the net. You might want to ask them what they like doing best, which are their favourite sites, things they don't like about it and whether they've had any uncomfortable experiences while on the web.

 'I hadn't a clue what was going on so I got my son to show me what he did on the net. I learnt a lot more from him than I would have from any book or website.' Linda, mum of boy aged 10

There are also a lot of good sources of information and advice on net safety for parents. Make the most of them. They vary widely – some are clearly aimed just at parents and go into a great amount of detail, others are for kids and adults and are both informative and fun (*see list on pages 206–207*).

2. Get your child web savvy

In the same way that kids know what might happen if they don't look before crossing the road, or if they go off with strangers, try and make them aware of the possible dangers of the net. If you share with them what your worries are, then they're more likely to be careful themselves.

Sometimes kids listen more if it's somebody else giving them advice rather than their parents. So, you might want to visit with your child some of the websites aimed at kids that spell out what the dangers of the internet are, and the best precautions to take. A good site to visit is www.chatdanger.com. This tells the story, for example, of one girl who ended up being hurt by a man she met in a chat room. Another popular site is For Kids by Kids Online at www.fkbko.co.uk

3. Control and monitor

There are things you can do to make your child's use of the net more safe. The most obvious thing is to install filtering software that blocks unsuitable content, as well as antivirus and firewall protection. But be careful, these blocking devices aren't perfect. Kids can resent being 'controlled' in this way, and so become motivated to beat the system. We came across lots of examples of children who had found ways around them.

Parents can also often get fed up with filtering systems because they either let through stuff they don't think should get through, or block stuff that they regard as completely harmless.

 'I gave up on our filter software in the end. It was stopping the most ridiculously harmless stuff and then letting really inappropriate stuff through. It was driving us all nuts.' *Stuart, dad of two boys.*

Another way to control what's going on, is to keep the internet screen somewhere in the house where you can easily keep an eye on it, for instance, in the living room or kitchen.

And if you want to keep your kids away from harmful content, try and direct them towards content that is educational, entertaining and appropriate for kids. Some parents use child-friendly sites like www.yahooligans.com or www.askjeevesforkids.com.

4. Encourage responsibility

Whatever you do, your kid's use of the internet will always be difficult to control completely. And even if you can keep control of their home usage, you won't necessarily be able to control how they use it elsewhere. Your kid, therefore, needs to share responsibility.

A good way of doing this is to sit down with your child and agree a 'Family Web Code' (see pages 204–205). Ideally this should be done before you allow your child to start using the internet, but whenever you do it, it's never too late.

The key to making the code a success is to explain the reasons behind the different rules.

5. Keep talking

Above all, keep talking to your child so that they feel comfortable about coming to you if they have any problems. Make it part of the daily routine to ask them what they've been doing on the internet. And do it in such a way that it doesn't sound as if you're snooping, but genuinely interested in what they've been up to.

If they have done something they shouldn't have, or been exposed to something inappropriate, don't overact. The most important thing is that you both keep talking and work together to solve any problems.

An example of a Family Web Code

Don't give out any personal information – for instance, your name, email address, postal address, phone number, photo, school address, or even your hobbies – without permission.
Reason: you don't know where this information will end up or how it will be used.

Be cautious with anyone you meet on the net.
Reason: they may not be who they say they are and their intentions may not be good.

Don't believe everything you read on the internet.
Reason: there is a lot of unreliable information on the net.
Kids are very trusting of anything printed – so you need to explain that just because it's printed it doesn't mean that it's true. It's also important to explain to kids that there are a lot of self-publicists and fraudsters about. A lot of internet material is nothing more than cheap advertising, while other material may be deliberately trying to deceive the reader. Kids needs to be taught how to check out sources – show them how to do a bit of detective work before accepting things as true.

Only respond to emails or instant messages from people – or addresses – you know.
Reason: they may contain viruses or horrible messages.

Let mum or dad know if you're concerned about anything or anyone that you've come across on the web.
Reason: it's better to share any problems because mum and dad might be able to help you.

Never arrange to meet anyone you've met on the web without talking to mum or dad first.
Reason: You might think you know them, but they are in fact complete strangers.

Don't step into territory that doesn't feel right. If you get sent an obscene message, for instance, don't be tempted to explore further. Or, if you accidentally end up on a dodgey web site take the exit rather than reading on.

Reason: Using the internet is all about trust. If mum and dad can't trust where you are going then they will stop you from using it. And thanks to the history/memory facilities on the computer they can check up on where you are going.

But, most, importantly help you child understand why it is best not to dig into inappropriate territory. There is a lot of nasty stuff out there – put up by people who want to shock adults and kids alike. You let those people win the day if you delve into their worlds.

Tips on blocking devices

- If you're looking for a simple solution on how to block inappropriate content, be prepared – there isn't one. While filtering products can be good, they are not foolproof and there is no substitute for parental involvement.

- Choose your Internet Service Provider carefully. Some provide educational material, safety information or protective software. Others do very little.

- Think carefully about what you want any filtering software to do. There are lots of different safety features ranging from those which control content, contacts or shopping to those which ensure privacy, improve your computer's security or monitor, record and stop internet activity.

- If you want detailed advice on what filtering product to get visit www.getnetwise.org. The site lists what filtering products are available and allows you to search for whatever feature interests you. Another useful site is www.pin.org.uk which is run by the Parents Information Network. This evaluates different filtering software available for parents.

Tips on safe chat

- Encourage your child to use 'child friendly' chat rooms. The good ones, for instance, will have a moderator to block any personal details being swapped and keep the chat suitable.

- If your child is visiting a chatroom, encourage them to keep to the public area where everyone can see the conversation and they should be safe.

- Check that your child's Internet Provider is also child friendly. Does it, for instance, provide information about what to do with unwanted messages, and easy to use ignore and block buttons?

- Above all, keep personal information personal. So don't give away any details about yourself when you go, for instance, to chat rooms or visit bulletin boards.

USEFUL WEBSITES FOR BECOMING WEB SAVVY

www.getnetwise.org
GetNetWise is a service provided by internet companies and public interest groups. It provides advice on internet use including safety on-line; stopping unwanted emails and Spam; protecting computers from hackers and viruses, and how to keep your personal information private.

www.kidsmart.org.uk
Kidsmart, which is produced by the children's internet charity Childnet, is a practical internet safety advice website for children, parents and schools.

www.chatdanger.com
Chatdanger, produced by Childnet International, is a site specifically for kids outlining the potential dangers of interactive services online such as chat, IM, online games, email and mobiles.

www.parentscentre.gov.uk
Parents Centre has been developed by The Department for Education and Skills. It provides advice on internet safety ranging from how to protect your child from pornography and paedophiles, to safe shopping on the internet and what to look out for when buying a computer.

www.iwf.org.uk

Internet Watch Foundation provides an authorized hotline for anyone to report illegal content on the internet. It also provides practical information on internet safety including safe surfing and how to go about choosing filter software.

www.fkbko.co.uk

For Kids by Kids Online (FKBKO) provides advice and information for kids on safe surfing.

www.bbc.co.uk

The BBC site offers a Webwise Online Course. This is very comprehensive and explains the basics of how the internet works.

www.thinkuknow.co.uk

Thinkuknow is a cartoon-based website from the Home Office which has advice on safe internet surfing.

www.nch.org.uk

The National Children's Home charity has a website which advises on internet safety for children.

Kids' tricks on the net

'Mum only lets me go on the CBeebies site. I wait for her to go into the dining room and then I go where she doesn't see me.' *9 year old girl*

'I go to a teens site. It's just gossip about bands that aren't really suitable for younger kids. When there are swearing songs, my mum doesn't really like that – I just minimize the screen when she comes in the room.' *8 year old girl*

For more information go to
www.mediadietforkids.com

 'In chat rooms I'm allowed to type in fake stuff, but no real details.'
9 year old girl

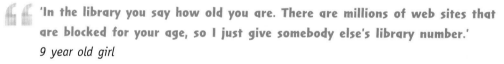 'In the library you say how old you are. There are millions of web sites that are blocked for your age, so I just give somebody else's library number.'
9 year old girl

 'When I was at school I went on eBay by accident.' 11 year old boy

'We put sex and things on other people's memories.' 12 year old boy

Chapter 10

Problems and solutions — controlling content

Subscribing to multi-channel services

'I've resisted subscribing to a multi-channel TV service because I'm frightened that it'll put too many temptations in front of the kids, and I'll loose control. Is this right?'

 Tips:

- There is a danger that things get out of control when there's so much to watch. So when you're new to a multi-channel service it's important to keep a close eye on how the kids use it. It's also important to set any ground rules firmly at the beginning.

- Parents with 5 to 9 year olds need to watch out for the cartoon channels. These can be a terrific draw in homes that have just got the service, and not surprisingly cartoon consumption amongst this age group tends to go up.

- With older kids it's obviously important to keep them away from the adult channels, and several parents told us how they particularly objected to some of the content on the music channels. They thought that the language and images of contemporary music culture can often be too aggressive and sexually explicit for young children.

- But the biggest temptation for adults and kids on the multi-channels is sport. In fact 9 out of the top 10 programmes in multi-channel homes are football-based programmes. This is territory that can be difficult for mum to control so when it comes to football, it is particularly important to set out the ground rules early on.

- But overall, the multi-channel services can bring enormous benefits to the home – it's just a question of keeping things in control. There are fantastic channels specifically aimed at younger children. CBeebies and The Disney Channel, for instance, are particularly good for pre-school kids. In fact, through sticking to these channels parents are given greater control over what their kids watch.

- Furthermore, there are now services like Sky⁺ and TiVo that allow parents to be more selective in what they watch. Sky⁺ allows parents to select programmes to be videoed at the beginning of the week, so that parents and kids together can devise their own personal schedule (*see section about TV Planning – page 166*).

Purchasing computer games

'How do I know when it's the right time to buy a new computer game?'

 Tips:

- Don't spoil your child with too many games. We spoke to one dad who proudly told us that he had bought the family 34 games over the last couple of years. He then told us that he had had a real problem with one of his sons who had become addicted to the screen. Some kids find it hard to cope when there's so much on offer.

- Let your child get bored with existing games before introducing any new ones into the home. It'll give them a cooling off period away from the computer when they can go off and do other things.

- Read our separate section on Buying Computer Games *(see page 170)*.

Play dates away

'How do I handle visits to friends? My son has one particular friend who has older brothers and sisters. I know when he goes round to his place they watch all these 18 rated channels and play violent computer games.'

 Tips:

- If you can, talk to the friend's parents about your concerns and see whether they're happy to keep some control on the situation when your son goes round.

- If you're still unhappy, try and get them to play more at your place where you have more control.

- Try and encourage your son to monitor his own media activity, and give him the confidence to tell his friend that he'd prefer to do something else.

- Keep the lines of communications with your son open. So, don't go beserk if he tells you they saw something inappropriate. Instead, explain why you think it is inappropriate for him.

Exposure to disturbing content

'How should I handle my child if he has seen something disturbing?'

 Tips:

- If your child is disturbed about something they have seen, first of all try and get a clear picture of what exactly is upsetting them. Don't be afraid to ask them specific questions about it.

- Then try and get your kid to feel more comfortable with the bad thoughts. You can do this in a number of ways, for instance, explaining why the situation is so unreal, or why it is most unlikely to happen. We spoke to one nanny who had just reassured a 4 year old about the scary dragon in Shrek.

 'I explained to her that it was just a game that the film makers were playing with us. I told her that they wanted us to be a little bit scared, because that made it really exciting to watch. I also told her that there were lots of things I get scared about when I watch films. Knowing that it was only a game and that she wasn't the only one to get scared made her feel a lot better.'
Emma, nanny of a 2 and 4 year old

- Finally, try and get your kid to forget the vision altogether. Encourage them to dump their thoughts in an imaginary dustbin, or simply get your kid thinking about other things. One mum told us how her daughter had a little book by her bed. If she has something on her mind they'll write it down in the book together. This acted as an effective debriefing exercise, or in other words, it was her daughter's 'scary thought dustbin'.

Films and books – which to encourage first?

'If there's a film of a children's book, should you hold off taking your child to see the film until they've read the book?'

 Tips:

- In an ideal world, yes. It's often a good incentive for a child to read, if you say that you'll take them to see a film once they've finished the book. It also ensures that your child puts their own imagination to work, rather than just being presented with all the fantasy and images on a plate. They then have the fun of either agreeing or disagreeing with the way things are shown in the film.

- But if your child can't read the book first, try and use the film itself as an incentive to read the book. They can still have fun discussing with you what they think worked, or didn't, in the film.

Screen exercise

'I've heard about dance mats and exercise routines that you can do in front of the screen – do they really address the problem of getting children off the couch.'

 Tips:

- We found that there was great enthusiasm for dance mats and exercise programmes, and they certainly appeared to be getting children moving in some households. If you get one, it's fun to set up a family league – these are games that everyone can join in.

- But do they really give you proper exercise? Well that's up to you – it's certainly possible to build up a sweat if you put your mind to it. But don't let it replace a walk down to the playground – there's no substitute for a bit of fresh air.

Games with cameras

'My son wants an Eye Toy but I am not certain that I like the idea of him starring in beat 'em ups on screen.'

 Tips:

- There are a number of programmes that incorporate the player into the game on screen. In the case of the Eye Toy the camera sits on top of the TV, and in other cases voice recordings are made direct into the computer.

- Does it matter that the distinction between reality and fantasy becomes too blurred? It really just depends on what the game involves. Think back to the key questions – what is the game getting my child to do, and what world do they enter? One father described an Eye Toy game where his son had to pretend to be a window cleaner. The son had a laugh and totally exhausted himself washing the imaginary windows.

- With the fighting games, just look carefully at the imagery. Check you feel happy with it before you get it. And if you do get it, keep a close eye on how the game affects your child's behaviour.

Mobile phones with cameras

'I have heard that school children are misusing cameras on mobile phones. Is this a real problem?'

 Tips:

- Yes, the mobile phone camera can become another tool for bullies and immature pranksters.

- We heard of a headmaster who had just told a group of parents that they had become his big problem this year. He described how bullies were using them to take demeaning pictures of other class mates. The pictures are then emailed to the rest of the school, or put up on a web site for the world to see. The cameras are also being used to send and create pornographic pictures.

- It's easy to understand why these new phones are a threat as well as a wonderful opportunity for kids. They fit in your pocket, it doesn't cost anything to take a photo and then it's as easy as can be to post your photo to the world. It's important that parents and kids recognize the dangers. So, if you decide to give your child one – keep in touch with how they are using it – and ensure that they understand that you will take it away if they misuse it.

Age-appropriate viewing

'My youngest son always ends up watching what his older brother has chosen. Should I worry about this?

 Tips:

- Yes, it is very important that children don't just watch programming that is targeted at older children and adults. A review commissioned by The Literary Trust shows that children can suffer as a result of watching too much programming that goes over their heads.[28] There is so much good programming specially targeted at younger children – check that you allow your little ones to benefit from it.

- See section on film and computer game ratings *(page 168)*.

Watching something again and again

'My 5-year-old wants to watch the same video time and time again. Is this s problem?

 Tips:

- It just depends on the quality and educational value of the video. Research shows that repeat viewing of quality videos can help a child's language development.[28] 'Quality' means videos that have some kind of educational element to them, or simply videos that have rich, yet simple, storylines and that introduce the child to new vocabulary. According to research young children benefit more from direct 'one to one' communication styles, rather than programming that floods them with information from lots of different directions.[28]

Step 2 – Summary

- An effective diet isn't just about cutting down, it's also about improving the quality of what you consume.

- Step 2 of The Media Diet is about improving the quality of your children's media consumption. The key here is not just looking at programme content, but more importantly your children's response to that content. Individual TV programmes and computer games will have different effects on children. It's important that you're aware of how your child is being influenced.

- Remember **'quality response = quality time'**.

- This section of the diet introduces the concept of 'media parenting skills'. It shows you how to develop media antennae to judge how your child is responding to different programmes.

- Checking out The 7 Responses is a practical formula for deciding whether a programme should or shouldn't be included into a child's media schedule. It's a way of helping you make the right media choices for your children. And in a digital world with so much choice, it's all the more important to choose well.

From media addiction to media substitutes — balancing media in your child's life

BALANCING MEDIA IN A CHILD'S LIFE

- Encouraging activity away from the screen
- Our recipe – 6 ingredients for time away from the screen

To cut down on your child's media consumption, you need to get them away from the screen. And that means finding good media substitutes to fill the void once the switch is turned off. If you can do this, you'll also help prevent the whole 'switching off' experience becoming a negative one.

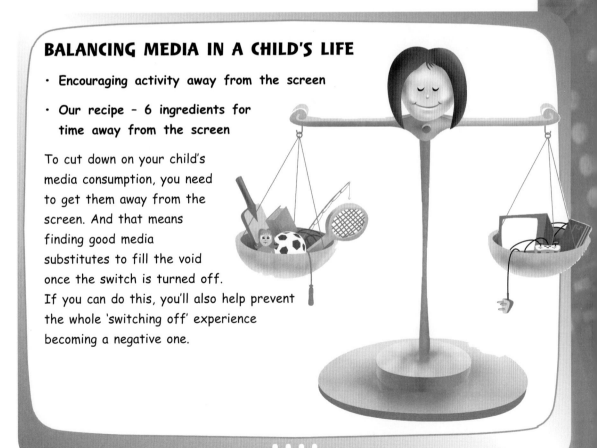

Chapter 11

Encouraging activity away from the screen

So, what non-screen activities should you be encouraging? And how can you do this in a way that isn't too time consuming for you?

Once again, we've developed this part of the diet with the help of our research group of over 100 parents, kids, grandparents, carers, teachers and children's experts. We asked them their views and tips on the subject. Many of the mums had interesting and useful things to say. But we found, in this particular area, that it was the grannies and carers who had some of the best advice to give.

We also tapped into Teresa's experience of the toy market. Once you know what makes a good toy, you have a pretty good understanding of what motivates children to play at home. And motivation is often the name of the game.

Like the rest of the diet, this section is deliberately simple and easy to follow. To start with, here are a bunch of general thoughts about encouraging kids' activity away from the screen.

1. Become more time smart

The grannies and carers particularly noticed how time-pressed mums have difficulty in setting time priorities. They recognised that mums today are very busy, but there was a general feeling that mums aren't always as time-efficient as they could be.

So, as mums, maybe we need to make sure we're more time smart. This doesn't necessarily mean spending more time on our children, but being more effective with how we use our time.

Here are some ideas about how to do this.

First of all, there's 'starter time'

If you want your child to get going on an activity they often need encouragement and – more often than not – your attention. It's worthwhile investing properly in 'starter time' at the beginning of any new activity.

So, rather than setting something up and then quickly leaving your child to get on with it, stop. Take some time out from what you're doing to get involved in the activity too. An extra five minutes of your time at the start, will help make the activity a success. Your child will play longer and you'll end up having more time to yourself.

And then there's 'nurture time'

You need to invest in a bit of nurture time too. Once your child's properly set up doing an activity, you can get on with something else. But keep popping back for another five minutes here or there to see how they're doing.

Children often just need little bits of encouragement to keep them going. Once they've decided that they're bored of a game, that's it. It's difficult to drum up enthusiasm again. And if that happens, you'll then have to spend more time getting them started on something else.

Being 'time smart' is about being flexible

If your child is happily playing or doing something, don't interrupt them if you don't have to. Go with the flow. Let whatever they're doing come to a natural end and make the most of the extra little bit of time you now have.

And finally, don't under value your time. It's a precious commodity. It's what your children want most of all. Five minutes away from chores is five minutes well spent.

 'All children want from the beginning is your time. And that's all they need. It's not toys, it's just you being there.' *Anne, granny of eight grandchildren*

2. Seed ideas – don't impose them!

Become a good 'seeder' of ideas, rather than always imposing ideas on your children. Children are the same as adults. If they feel they've had an idea, they'll pursue it better than if they think it's somebody else's. So, don't be proud. Encourage your child to take ownership of your ideas.

Give your child activity options and let them then take it from there. Things may not develop quite how you imagined – in fact they probably won't. But then it doesn't really matter. Be prepared for some of your ideas to fall on deaf ears. Sometimes ideas quickly take root, and on other occasions children just aren't in the mood. One day they'll be mad on doing one thing, and the next they'll reject it just like that.

So, don't be dogged with ideas that haven't inspired your child. Just drop them and keep them up your sleeves for another day. But above all, listen out for their ideas and only suggest things to do if you need to.

The kids often come up with the best ideas

221

3. Develop 'themes'

In the mid eighties the big talk in children's marketing was all about 'concept marketing' and 'multi-media' strategies. It sounds like a whole lot of jargon but the ideas were simple. Instead of selling 'one off' toys you developed 'a concept' which was often based on a character in a film. You then flogged it across as many different markets as you could.

Teresa says:

'I was working on the launch of My Little Pony in the UK. We pursued a 'concept marketing' strategy to good effect. There was an advertising campaign that established the fantasy around the concept. The commercials acted as mini films and Hywel Bennett told the stories. We supported the television with different media, such as comics, and developed a range of merchandise. Stationery, food, clothes – you name it – they had 'My Little Pony' on them.

In the boys' market, Teenage Mutant Turtles were having equal success. Sylvanian Families, Cabbage Patch, Power Rangers and more recently Harry Potter, Shrek and Bratz are all examples of the success of concept marketing.'

Now, turning to our families – how can we put the tricks of concept marketing to good effect? The first thing is to identify a theme which is captivating your child. This might be a film, TV show, song, story from a book or a family big event. Then have fun thinking how you can develop the theme.

We found that carers were instinctively doing this.

One carer described how she and her children had all been singing 'The Toothbrush' song on the way home. Once inside, they painted a picture of a toothbrush and then made a giant toothbrush to play with. It might have been a mad song but it provided a great theme for an afternoon's activity.

Another carer described how her children were currently captivated by the video of the musical, Oliver. They love acting out the songs and having a go at the dance routines. She encouraged them to put together a show. It kept them busy for hours as they rehearsed and then performed it to their family and friends.

Other themes we came across that fuelled play and creativity for the day were princes and princesses, weddings, going on holiday and favourite films. The list could go on and on because there's no end to what children find captivating.

TV and computer games are a rich source of inspiration for activity themes. Make the most of them.

4. Encourage hobbies and interests

We noticed in our research that it was often children with interests or hobbies who had the most balanced approach to watching the TV and playing on the computer.

'My youngest son is very musical, he plays an instrument. He's more outgoing than the other. I can't see computer games ever being a problem with him'. *Anna, mum of three*

These children also often speak with pride about what they do away from the screen.

'I only play about one hour on the PlayStation because then I have to go diving. If I'm not diving, I'm dancing.' *9 year old girl*

We also came across several cases where a child had become addicted to the screen, and the parents had managed to solve the problem by finding something else to interest them.

'We were buying him games and he would be on them day after day. So we started looking for a hobby. It was an accident in the end. He went with his school to a weekend adventure thing and discovered he was good at archery. Luckily enough we found there was a local archery place, and now we take him to it four times a week.' *Neil, dad, car mechanic*

223

There was another example of a single mum who was worried her daughter was spending too much time on the internet and computer. She encouraged her daughter to get a hobby. Eventually she started working for a local riding stables in her spare time. Looking after the horses gave the girl a great sense of purpose. It also made her feel part of a local community.

Chapter 12

Our recipe — 6 ingredients for time away from the screen

6 INGREDIENTS TO ENCOURAGE ...

- Chat
- Reading
- Creativity and music
- Exercise
- Helping around the home
- And above all, PLAY!

 for quality time away from the screen

Our recipe

We asked our research groups what activities they would advise first time parents to encourage their kids to do away from the screen. We wanted them to advise on activity areas which would provide a healthy balance in a kid's life.

They identified 6 key areas:

- chat
- reading
- creativity and music
- exercise
- helping around the home
- play

And, when you think about it, it makes total sense. Between them, these six activity areas provide some of the essential ingredients for creating a happy and healthy child. They also give your child a useful jumping off point for the future. If they're used to this mixture of activities in the early years, they'll be more likely to get the balance right as an adult.

Encouraging your child to love exercise isn't, for instance, just about controlling their current waistline. It's about giving them a love for exercise and a habit that they can take on into adulthood. Likewise, play isn't just about entertaining a child now. It will encourage them to interact with others, and help them tap into their inner initiative and resourcefulness.

So, focus on encouraging these 6 activity areas. Think of them as essential ingredients in a child's lifestyle diet. Try and ensure that your child gets a good all round balance.

As we know that's easier said than done. For a start, if you're anything like us there are probably certain things you like doing with your children better than others.

Teresa says:

'I love kicking a football about with the boys. I feel less of a star when it comes to sitting down and reading – and as for helping with music practice, I fail hopelessly.'

Louise says:

'I also enjoy anything outdoors. The swings, bicycling, running or playing hide and seek. That's all great – I'm there doing it with them. I'm not so good at being cooped up indoors.'

It was obvious when we talked to mums that they also enjoyed doing certain things, and weren't so keen on others.

There's an easy way to get round this. Just be honest with yourself. What aren't you so good at encouraging your child to do? If you're not so enthusiastic about one activity area, can you get your partner more involved? Or, perhaps it's an activity area which your child can be encouraged to pursue with friends.

Thoughts on the 6 ingredients

Here are some specific thoughts about how to encourage children to become involved in the six activity areas. Think of them as a bundle of ideas. You'll probably have loads more yourself, but these were the ones which our research team thought were the most important and helpful.

And, because this is above all a media book and we're two media enthusiasts, we pay special attention to ways of using the media itself to encourage each activity area.

Ingredient 1 – Chat

It's important for all sorts of reasons that children learn to talk and have proper conversations. It helps them socially because they can articulate their own feelings and views, and interact with others. Many of the parents in our research complained about a generation of grunters who have to resort to physical actions in order to express themselves.

'Kids can find it hard to communicate. If they can't express themselves, they go straight for the physical.' *Sharon, nanny with two children*

If a child is articulate, it also helps them academically because they're able to take a full part in the learning experience. They can ask and answer questions and follow a line of debate. Being a good talker, also gives any child a much needed boost in confidence. So, the more we talk and chatter to our kids, the better. It doesn't matter if we don't have something important to say. We should be talking to them about anything and everything – the weather, what we're doing, what they've done or simply how they're feeling.

And the grannies in our research highlighted the importance of not rushing children if you want a proper chat. Children often just need time to respond and will give their best responses after a moment of reflection. So, try not to hurry them.

'If you want a proper conversation with a child, you can't go charging in there. You do it slowly. What did you do today? Did you have a good day? How was Hannah? And slowly you'd be surprised at what comes out. They won't tell their mum about the bullies – I'm the one who picks it up.' *Sylvia, granny with three grandchildren*

Top tips from our research ...

Establish a 'catch-up' routine

Make 'catch up moments' part of your daily routine. Let your child know that at certain times of day – on the way back from school, at tea or after the bedtime story – they'll have your undivided attention. Use this time to chat and find out what they've been doing and how they're feeling. Don't worry if it's only five minutes here or there – it's better than nothing.

'With children a lot of the things that are going on are little things, which you can only pick up when you have a moment quietly with them.'
Jane, granny with four grandchildren

'In the evening when they go to bed, when you read them a story, it's quiet time then, and you can chatter about the day. If they know they have that time with you, if there's a problem, they can work it out with you, because you're used to talking to each other.' *Helen, nanny with two children*

Don't be put off by a 'grunt'

A lot of parents talked to us about 'grunting' kids who were difficult to communicate with. If you get a grunt from your child, or a monosyllabic yes or no, it's probably because they don't feel you're on their wavelength.

Think carefully about how you phrase questions. If one approach doesn't work, try a different way of asking the same question.

'They all just talk like "grunt, grunt, grunt". It's hard to get anything out of them.' *Elsa, mum from inner city*

Question and imagine

Children like to be asked about themselves, so ask them questions even if you know the answers. Sometimes their responses and comments won't make total sense. Be patient and use your imagination to find out what they're really trying to tell you.

'Kids can suddenly say something that makes no sense at all. They might out of the blue start talking about space ships. It's up to you to explore what they are trying to say and why. Sometimes you need quite a lot of imagination to fathom out what they are going on about.' *Head teacher*

Make meal times, chat times

In many homes the family meal is under threat because of the TV. As a result parents and children don't regularly sit around the table and talk to one another.

Try and use meal times as an opportunity for everyone in the family to catch up on the day's events. It should be a relaxing moment when you can all enjoy a good

229

chat. And even if you don't eat with your children, get a cup of tea and sit down with them.

 'At tea time, you're finding out what everybody's been doing during the day. If you put the telly on, you can't find out anything because nobody's talking.' *Granny with three grandchildren*

Use songs

Songs are a great way of getting kids to be expressive and remember words. Sing along with your children whenever you can – doing the cooking, at bath time or walking to school.

 'We're always singing songs in the car. Those kiddie tapes drive me mad, but they're great for getting them remembering things.' *Julie, nanny with three kids*

Consider getting a pet

Pets can encourage kids to develop strong relationships in their lives. Children are often still happy to talk to their pets, even when they don't seem in the mood to talk to anyone else.

WHY PETS ARE A GREAT ASSET

Someone to ...

... talk to (when I'm fed up with everyone else)
... play with (he gets me outside)
... care for (with a little help from mum)
... indulge (if he does a trick for me)
... be quiet with (he shares my thoughts)

 A great diversion away from the screen

Use the media to ...

Chatter about the TV and computer games

Modern media provides loads of things for you to chat about. So, for instance, discuss the story lines of the soaps with your child, the characters of a film or even the best ways of playing a particular computer game.

'I went swimming with the girls today, and they were all talking about East Enders. It's difficult because it's not always very good viewing for 10 year olds, but it's what they all talk about at school.'
Fran, mum with 10 year old girl and 13 year old boy

Debate moral and social issues

Use what your child has seen in the soaps, or on the news, as a stimulus for discussion. Listen to their views and encourage them to develop their own thoughts

'There was the teenage pregnancy in East Enders. It was a good opportunity for me to sit down with my daughter and chat about those sorts of things – what did she think of it, what would she do in a similar situation. Because it was one step removed it made it easier to chat about.'
Lucy, mother with 9 year old girl

Teresa says:

'I had an example where the news gave us all a great subject for debate. Chris had seen the crowds storming the Parliament building in Azerbaijan and came running into the kitchen to tell me. He was captured by the crowd scenes and the drama of it all.

I got Chris to tell his dad what had happened at supper. This led to a family discussion about the introduction of democracy in the Soviet Union and then to the issue of postal voting in the UK. I asked the kids what they thought of the new reforms. Both Isabel and Christopher were really engaged in the conversation and enjoyed giving their views on world issues.'

Our recipe – 6 ingredients for time away from the screen

Build friendships

It goes without saying that encouraging friendships is an important way of getting kids to talk, and modern media has so much to offer when it comes to social networks.

Encourage children from the age of about 9 to use email, MSN and texting as a way of keeping in contact with friends and family.

> 'I text my aunt on my mobile. I just ask her how she is and things like that.'
> *Jack, aged 10*

Encourage family viewing

Even if you all have TVs in your separate bedrooms, try and watch programmes together rather than allowing 'satellite' viewing – where everybody watches in their own personal space. We spoke to one mum who made it a rule that no one could watch TV in their room if they were all watching the same thing. It's more social because you can then talk about what you've all watched.

> 'If there's a programme that we are all going to watch, like EastEnders, then if it's on downstairs, they come and watch it with us.'
> *Karen, mum with 2 kids, each has TV in their room*

> 'The TV in her room is not connected to the aerial, deliberately, so she can just watch videos. So she doesn't watch TV on her own, it can be quite isolating. We cuddle up on the sofa. Snuggle in and watch together.'
> *Nikky, with 10 year old daughter*

Ingredient 2 – Reading

Learning to read takes time and it often requires a lot of patience from parents to inspire children with a love of reading. But it's worth the effort. If a child gets behind in reading they quickly get behind in their schoolwork. And if a child enjoys reading, they find a whole new world opening up before them.

The teachers we spoke to stressed the importance of making reading something fun to do, rather than something which is just done at school or as part of the homework. And if your child is a reluctant reader, the advice from the teachers is that some reading is better than no reading at all. So, let them read Beano, Girl Talk or the sports pages of the newspapers – if that's what they want. At least your child's reading.

 ## Top tips from our research ...

Read with your children – whatever their age

Start reading with your children at an early age to encourage a love of books and stories. And don't presume it's only the little ones who enjoy being read to. The older ones do as well. So, for example, try reading spy stories to a 9 year old boy, or fashion magazines to a 12 year old girl.

A good way of encouraging children to read is to share the reading. Take it in turns to read different bits. You can read one page – or even one sentence – and your child can read the next. Or, make it fun, with you being one character and your child being another.

Have a good selection of reading material

Build up a love of reading by having a good choice of books for your children to dip in and out of. Encourage your child to pick and choose the books they want.

Having a good selection of books needn't cost money. Make the most of your local library and any school books. Try and involve your child in choosing which books to have. Libraries and bookshops can be inspiring for kids and great places to entertain them for the odd hour or so.

If you need advice about what good books to get, ask other parents or teachers at school, and staff at your local library or bookshop. There are also a number of good book guides – for example, *The Ultimate Book Guide* by Anne Fine and *The Rough*

Guide to Children's Books by Nicholas Tucker – as well as organisations, such as The Book Trust (www.booktrust.org.uk), which provide lists of popular books.

End the day with a bedtime story

Try and read to your child last thing at night. This is where dads, in particular, can play an important role. A lot of families make bedtime stories dad's special time. If dad has been out at work it's something easy and enjoyable he can do with the kids before they go to bed.

But remember, reading isn't just for bedtime. Encourage your child to read five minutes here, and five minutes there, throughout the day.

END THE DAY WITH A BEDTIME STORY

Make the most of interests and hobbies

Sometimes kids get bored with reading because they're simply not interested in what they're reading. Get books and reading material connected with hobbies and things that interest your child.

This is particularly important with boys, who aren't always natural readers. They often find non-fictional reading matter more interesting than fiction. Football and science magazines, for example, are great because they grab their attention and get them reading.

Start a family 'book club'

If you've got an 11 or 12 year old, suggest to them that they choose a book for you both to read. You can then have fun discussing it, and the characters, with them.

 ## Use the media to …

Learn to read

There are great computer programmes that help kids develop their reading skills (*see Educational Games section page 175*), and sitting at a screen can offer kids a welcome break from school reading books.

 'We use the DK Learning Ladder. It's got a bit of everything to support Key Stage 1 and 2. It's a good way of supplementing homework and makes the whole learning experience more appealing.' Carolyn, mum and part-time teacher

Read around a favourite media theme

Make use of supporting comics, books and web-sites for television or computer programmes.

 'Rachel watches Angelina Ballerina sometimes and I've had to buy all the books. She's five and she will try hard to read them. It's been a way of getting her into reading.' *Liz, mum with daughter aged 5*

235

Read up around factual TV programmes and series

Factual programmes often inspire a sudden interest and enthusiasm for a particular subject. Make the most of the moment. Encourage reading around the subject – either by visiting any supporting website, or getting books on the subject from the library.

Get reading on the internet

Surfing the internet involves reading all the time, and it can be a great way of encouraging a lazy reader to get motivated. Visiting sites about their favourite passions and interests makes them want to read – suddenly they realize that being able to read can be really useful. (*See Family Web Code on page 204.*)

Read the book of the film

Films are often good ways of inspiring interest in particular books, such as the Harry Potter books and *Lord of the Rings*. Make the most of your child's interest in a film by encouraging them to read the book.

Read newspapers to complement what's been on TV

It's often more interesting reading about things if they're topical. Encourage your child to read the newspaper to find out more about what they've seen on TV – for instance, football reports or news items.

Foreign newspapers can be a good source for encouraging language learning. Explore the foreign news options on the internet with your child and get in the habit of printing off features that might be of interest. For instance, football articles for the boys and music features for the girls.

Visit the great selection of book-related sites on the internet

There are lots of sites which are reading related, such as www.bbc.co.uk/arts/books. Encourage your child to visit these sites to find out about authors and books.

Ingredient 3 - Creativity and music

Everybody's talented and so it's important to try and seek out and encourage your child's creative strengths. If your child finds they're particularly good at something, the likelihood is that they'll become passionate about it too. You might be surprised by what you find. Just because you're no good at music, for instance, doesn't necessarily mean your child won't be either.

A lot of the teachers we spoke to commented that parents often stifle any potential creativity in their children by not giving them enough time and space. We try and cram too much into a day, rushing from one planned activity to another. As one teacher said, it's good for children occasionally to be left to their own devices because that's when they start to become very creative.

 Top tips from our research ...

Explore different forms of creativity

Help your child to explore their own creative potential by trying out different things. Look carefully, for instance, at what inspires your child to pick up a pencil and draw a picture, or start practicing the guitar. Find an instrument or artistic outlet that inspires them, rather than imposing on them what you want them to do.

 'Don't impose ideas on a child. You have to listen to what they are saying. If they don't like doing something you can't force it.' Charlotte, child carer

Expose kids to different types of instruments and music – classical, pop, bagpipes, jazz, army bands, African, Indian and Chinese. And show your child a variety of forms of art and styles – painting, sculpture, etching and mosaic, for instance.

Be spontaneous

Creativity should be spontaneous – don't just leave it for rainy days. So make sure your child has easy access to any art material – pens, papers, paints – or musical instruments. Your child can then easily, for example, start painting or making music. If everything is hidden away in cupboards and difficult to get to, the moment will pass and they'll be on to something else.

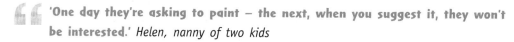

'One day they're asking to paint – the next, when you suggest it, they won't be interested.' *Helen, nanny of two kids*

Be an audience for your child's talents

If kids feel their work is being appreciated, they'll want to do more. Create a display area for art at home. Consider, for instance, laminating pictures and sticking them up on the kitchen wall. It's a cheap way to protect them and makes them look good too.

'There is a corner of our home which is just for her to display things. She's so proud of it.' *Alison, nanny of three kids*

Encourage your child, when they're ready, to play their latest pieces of music to the family and friends. Get them to put together little plays, and check you put time aside to come and watch.

Get your child to think visually

When asked how do you encourage artistic creativity in children, one art teacher immediately replied 'open their eyes'. She went on to explain how important it is that children learn how to look at the world around them.

'Parents should try and encourage their children to use their eyes more. If you're chatting with your child, get them to describe what they see in terms of shapes, colours, shades and textures. It's only by looking at things carefully that you can start to understand how to reproduce them in art.' *Sophie, art teacher*

Another teacher stressed the importance of art appreciation.

> 'The best way of getting kids interested in art is by getting them to notice it and comment on it. So, if you see a picture with your kid, get them to tell you what they see. Do they like the subject matter? Does it make them happy or sad? How would they have painted it?' *Hilary, mum and art teacher*

Make use of the different times of year

The different seasons of the year provide great opportunities to be creative. Encourage your child to make cards and decorations at Christmas or Chinese New Year; decorate pumpkins or cut out witches at Halloween and paint eggs and bunnies at Easter. Prepare lamps in the home for the Hindu festival of Diwali, the festival of light, or celebrations for the end of Ramadam.

Have fun with different materials

Put away the toys and leave your child with a large box of interesting items – old bits of materials, shoes or whatever – and see what they do.

Get them to look out for interesting boxes and packages that can be used to make things. Do collages and junk modelling with sweet wrappers, autumn leaves or old bits of newspaper. Make exotic jewellery with pasta or buttons, and try out old saucepans and spoons for musical instruments.

Make music practice part of the daily routine

One music teacher we spoke to said that music practice should be like brushing your teeth – in other words, doing it regularly is really what counts. So, five minutes a day is better than 20 minutes just before the next lesson.

Encourage art and music as a form of escapism

As kids get older art and music can increasingly provide them with light relief from the stresses and strains of the real world. This is something which should be encouraged.

Remember you are encouraging a hobby for life. It should be a pleasure rather than a chore. Don't let the pressures of exams spoil your child's love of music or art.

Use the media to ...

Get ideas and inspiration

There are some terrific TV programmes that encourage children to be creative – for example, Art Attack and Blue Peter. Visit the websites of these creative shows to get details of what's been shown on the screen.

> 'My kids do enjoy Art Attack. I love seeing what he is going to make.'
> *Christine, mum with two kids aged 5 and 7*

> 'There are things on the CBeebies website. Things to make. It's positive because if they've forgotten – it's on the website.'
> *Katherine, mum with two kids aged 6 and 9*

Popular light entertainment shows can be a great source of inspiration for getting the kids to perform themselves. For example, Pop Idol became a big inspiration at Isabel's school. Groups of girls got together in break time to practise being a pop group – and then they performed in front of their peers, who judged them.

HERE ARE SOME GIRLS PERFORMING THEIR VERSION OF POP IDOL

Get practical help and useful tools

The computer can provide a rich source of inspiration for writing, music, painting, arts and crafts. Explore software packages like Storyteller to help you become a film or cartoon producer, or Creative Writer to try your hand at being an author.

If your child is artistically inclined they can have fun with Adobe Photoshop, creating work a professional designer would be proud of. Or, they can go and be inspired by visiting the art galleries of the world – The Metropolitan, The National Gallery or The Louvre – all on the internet.

For musicians bored with practicing their grade pieces, there's a site called www.musicroom.com where you can download popular sheet music which is fun to play. Or you can develop your skills as a DJ by creating your own music compilation using a MP3 Player or ipod.

Teresa says:

'Isabel got an ipod Shuffle for her birthday. She has a long bus trip to school and we thought she would enjoy putting together her own music selections. She's had fun with it and it's made her more music savvy because she can actually choose the music herself.'

Encourage kids to enter competitions

There are lots of competitions on the TV. These can often be a useful focus and incentive for kids to get creative. There are also internet sites, such as www.bbc.co.uk/arts/books where kids are encouraged to send in work. Again this can inspire them into action.

Ingredient 4 – Exercise

We all know exercise is vital for a child's healthy development. Children and young people should do a minimum of 60 minutes of physical activity a day, and at least twice a week this should include more vigorous exercise to develop bone health and muscle strength.[16]

But kids today aren't exercising enough. In England and Scotland about 30 per cent of boys and 40 per cent of girls are not meeting the recommended activity guidelines.[47] One of the problems about modern living is our sedentary lifestyle. We drive or take the bus everywhere rather than walk. And a lot of sport is football focussed. So, if you're not good at football, people often presume you're not good at sports.

We spoke to one sports coach who highlighted the importance of kids trying out different sports and forms of exercise:

 'It's easy to be labelled not sporty if you don't like football. We try to involve them in a variety of sports like hockey, basket ball and archery. Then they can have fun trying things out – and if they are interested we find them a local club.' *Professional sports coach*

If your child shows no interest in football, don't give up. Explore other sports or exercise routines to get them interested and motivated.

 Top tips from our research ...

Get your child walking

The simplest way to get more exercise is to start walking more. If you can get somewhere on foot with your child, go there on foot. The more walking a child does, the better he or she will get at it – so get rid of the buggy as soon as you can.

WHATEVER THE SHAPE OF YOUR CHILD

Too much sedentary activity = a danger for their health

'I used to walk the little one to school and the teachers used to commend me, because all the other 5 and 6 year olds came in on the bus or in a car.' *Alison, nanny of two kids*

'If they're walking from an early age then they're quite happy to walk later on.' *Julie, nanny of three kids*

'As we walk we look at the trees, flowers, conkers. That's what children in front of the screen are missing.' *Helen, nanny with two kids*

Walking can be an entertaining activity in itself. So if you're walking to the shops, enjoy doing other things along the way – kicking the leaves, playing 'I spy', counting the yellow cars, or getting them to play your own fantasy game.

243

Teresa says:

Hugo invented a fantasy race game during a family walk through a wood. He pretended to be super fast Dash from The Incredibles, and each of us took it in turns to race him. We got back home in record time.

With older children let them lead the way and break up the journey looking at things of interest. But remember what you find interesting may not be the same as what interests them. You may want to stop to admire the view, while they may be interested in following a trail of ants.

Take your kids to the park or outside as much as possible

Children naturally want to run around and get outside. Give them the space to do it by taking them to the local park. If there isn't a park nearby, still try and give your child as much outside time as possible. Traffic permitting, let them enjoy some 'supervised' street life. You can keep an eye on them from the door or out of the window, as they ride their bike or go on their rollerblades.

Don't feel you have to play with your child all the time when you're outside. Look at your watch and divide your time ... half for them and half for yourself with a good book or newspaper.

244

Exercise with your children

One of the biggest incentives for any child to take exercise is to see their parents taking some form of exercise too. Use their exercise time as an opportunity for you to get some exercise too. As they change into their football shorts, put on your tracksuit and either join them in a game or go off and jog round the pitch. Likewise, if you take your kids swimming, grab the opportunity to do a few lengths yourself.

And don't let the weather stop all exercise. There are plenty of things that can be done inside – jumping around to children's exercise tapes, or visiting the local swimming pool.

Encourage your children to join an after-school or week-end sports club

These are a great and easy way for children to get exercise – particularly if you don't have very accessible outside space. And children – particularly the boys – love them because they turn sport into a social and competitive event. Playing for a team is fun, as well as giving kids an extra incentive to do well.

Encourage the competitive spirit

We asked a cricket coach to describe how he encouraged children's enthusiasm for the game. He believed that encouraging children to be competitive is a great way to get them motivated. Children enjoy being competitive – and it's easy for an adult to ensure that everybody feels a winner.

What's more, competitiveness isn't just about competing against other people. It's also about personal goal setting – and this is more important than anything.

 'Get the kids to be competitive. This may be against each other, or against themselves. Setting personal goals makes it fun for the kids. Make them believe that nobody is BAD at sport – it's just that some people are better than others.' *Professional county cricket coach*

Be an audience for kids as they play

Kids love an audience. Take time out to watch them do their sport. Comment on their new skills or tactics and give them the confidence to keep on going at it.

Involve dad as much as possible

A lot of dads particularly love sports – either watching them or doing them. Make the most of this natural enthusiasm and competitiveness to encourage a love of exercise in your kids.

 ## Use the media to ...

Play football after watching a match on TV

While they're still gripped in the excitement of the game, make the most of it. As soon as the match is finished, get them outside re-enacting bits of the game or just playing out their own fantasies.

Use big sporting events to inspire an interest in sport

Events like the Olympics or Commonwealth Games, which are broadcast on TV, or made into a computer game, are great opportunities to inspire an interest in a new sport.

Use them as much as you can. See which sport takes your child's fancy and then investigate the best ways of trying it out.

Encourage fantasy games

If your child is keen on a particular sport, try and get them to build fantasy worlds around it. This might involve becoming a commentator of a pretend football match, building pretend stadiums or practicing penalty shoot outs.

Find out more about sports

There are lots of good sites on the internet – such as www.bbc.co.uk/sportacademy – which can fuel an interest in a particular sport. The internet can also put you in touch with local or specialist communities following a particular sport. The football club sites are a classic examples.

Get dancing

You don't have to just sit in front of the screen. A lot of parents mentioned the dance mats and Eye Toys as great examples of how the screen can get kids to get up and exercise.

" 'The Dance Mat games. I'd let them play on that because they're active and they're interacting with their friends.' *Tracey, mum with 10 year old girl*

" 'Strictly Come Dancing. You see the costumes. It's lighthearted. And it inspires them to dance.' *Jennie, mum with two girls aged 8 and 10*

Ingredient 5 – Helping around the home

Most of us mums complain that children don't help enough around the home. Maybe, however, it's often our own fault for not encouraging them to do more. When we're short of time we often think it's easier and quicker to do the job ourselves.

It would certainly save us time in the long term if we got better at delegating. It would also help make sure our children have a sense of belonging to a family unit. Helping around the home can create a moment of togetherness and a good opportunity to chat. It also encourages kids to take on responsibility. If, for instance, they have to tidy up after a play, it makes them more conscious of the mess they're making.

Interestingly, it was single mums and mums with an only child, who had the best tips to pass on in this area. If you're a single mum it's particularly important that you work as a team with your children so you can share the responsibilities with them. And, an only child will often enjoy the companionship of being with mum or dad as they share a task together.

'We try and share the responsibilities in the house. I'll say, "mummy's been at work all day, so it's unfair if she has to do all the work". We try and share the ups and downs. My youngest says, "you sit down and I'll make you a cup of tea".' *Susan, single mum*

'I know it's hard but it's nice to try and involve them in the cooking – even though it can take longer and create a lot more mess.' *Sara, single mum*

Taking responsibility for particular jobs can also give children a sense of pride and confidence as they become part of the adult world.

'Even if they're just helping laying the table, clearing the table, or doing a little bit of housework. They feel they're doing something adult.' *Susan, single mum*

Top tips from our research

Make it fun

Try and make household tasks something fun that you all do together, rather than just a chore. So, for instance, have a good chat or sing song while you're making the beds, or run competitions to see who can finish their task the first, or do theirs the best.

Allocate ownership

Give specific household responsibilities to your child so that they feel a sense of ownership and pride. Make them, for instance, be in charge of sweeping the floor after tea, laying the table, washing up ... and, of course, tidying up their own mess.

If there are particularly unpopular jobs, consider introducing rotas for them.

Resist giving rewards

Try not to give rewards for little jobs around the house. Ideally, your child should do them as a matter of habit. The big jobs – like washing the car – are a different matter, however. If appropriate, give your child a bit of extra pocket money for helping out on these jobs.

Appreciate and admire

Don't take your child's help for granted. Make sure you stop and admire what they've done.

 ## Use the media to ...

Encourage an interest in the home

There are lots of TV programmes about household things – cooking, DIY and gardening, for instance. Watch them with your child and have fun seeing how the celebrity chefs and gardeners go about their tasks.

 'Mine are into Big Cook Little Cook. Gets them wanting to be chefs.'
Ellen, with two kids aged 4 and 6

Ingredient 6 – Play

Play is a critical part of childhood. Through play children discover themselves, their friends and the world. So, it's important that as parents we give our kids the space and time to play. We don't need to be there as a constant entertainer. We should occasionally just sit back and let them get on with it.
The earlier children start playing by themselves, the better they'll get at it.

'There are times when you have to step back. You can't be in control of them the whole time, you've just got to let them have fun playing at whatever they want.'
Jenny, child carer

'I don't think parents should do all the entertaining. One of the young mums at school said to me the other day, "you don't fuss over the children", and I said, "no, because, they've got to learn how to sort themselves out." You mustn't interfere too much. I say 'go and find something to play with", and after a whinge and a grizzle, they'll find something.' *Julia, Grandmum*

Toy manufacturers often use 'enduring play themes' when they're developing new toy concepts. These themes include caring; role play; good versus bad; construction; wheels and my little world. The reason why they're called 'enduring' is that they represent the psychological motivations that are at the heart of play. These are fundamental play characteristics that endure from one generation to the next, and that attract children to the most successful toys.

Louise says:

'If I look at my two daughters, their favourite play themes at the moment are 'caring' and 'role play'. They'll spend hours on end looking after their dolls and teddies. One of them will be the mummy and the other the daddy. Then they'll swap around, or become a doctor or nurse.'

As a parent it's useful to be aware of these different themes because it can help you understand what inspires a child to play. Try and ensure that your child has toys with a selection of different themes. And when you're putting toys away, think themes again. If the toys are in a muddle it makes it harder for a child to focus on any one activity.

 Top tips from our research ...

Develop play themes that can last for a couple of days

Encourage your kids to develop a theme that can act as a focus for a couple of days. This could involve building a setting for imaginative play, for instance, a Lego football pitch or a make-believe stadium for a pop concert. Forget about clearing up for a couple of days, and make the most of the centrepiece for all sorts of imaginary games.

ENDURING PLAY THEMES

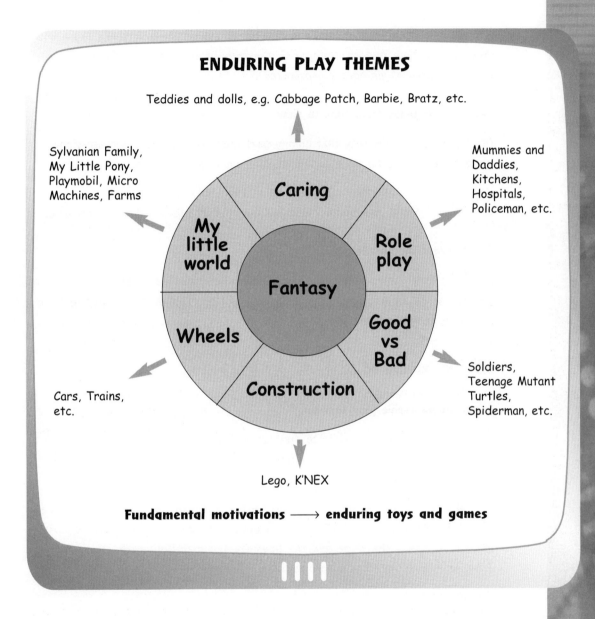

Teddies and dolls, e.g. Cabbage Patch, Barbie, Bratz, etc.

Sylvanian Family, My Little Pony, Playmobil, Micro Machines, Farms

Mummies and Daddies, Kitchens, Hospitals, Policeman, etc.

Caring

My little world

Role play

Fantasy

Good vs Bad

Wheels

Construction

Cars, Trains, etc.

Soldiers, Teenage Mutant Turtles, Spiderman, etc.

Lego, K'NEX

Fundamental motivations ⟶ enduring toys and games

Get your kid to improvise

Improvisation can be much more fun than ready bought toys. It also spurs on your child's powers of initiative. So, for example, help them make a cot for their favourite dolly out of a shoebox; use kitchen pans as musical instruments; build dens and camps in cupboards, and set up table tennis on the kitchen table.

251

'Jemma will come in and say, "I'm a Princess today, are you going to be a Queen?" And you just go along with the flow of what they're doing.'
Christine, nanny of girl aged 7 and boy aged 5

Let them be noisy from time to time

Don't throw the drum away that granny gave them for Christmas. The occasional noisy game is good for them and it allows them to let off steam.

 'Parents today don't like noisy games – if you buy them a drum, it soon disappears.' *Sylvia, grandmother who had given her grandson a drum for Christmas*

Don't forget the classic games

A lot of classic games like Snakes and Ladders, Monopoly, Battle Ships, Noughts and Crosses and Tiddly Winks have stood the test of time. Introduce your kids to them as well as trying out new ones.

➔ Use the media to ...

Inspire imaginative play themes

So, for instance, get your child to dress up as Sleeping Beauty after watching the video, play pirates after watching Pirates of the Caribbean, or start dancing after seeing Bombay Dreams.

 'We played a great pirate game after watching Pirates of the Caribbean. Each boy had a boat and a set of pirates. I used some cushions to create a series of islands across the floor and the boys started attacking each other. '
Anne, mum with three kids aged 6 to 12

Teresa says:

'I often use the themes of films to inspire fantasy play. We have just watched The Incredibles and Hugo has had fun in the garden pretending to race over a sea of water. He was sliding over a plastic sheet that we sprinkled with water and the vision of Dash charging over the sea kept him amused for half an hour.'

Inspire real action play

Game shows and big events can be an inspiration for real action. We came across a mum, for instance, who had created a challenge game after watching Raven.

Teresa says:

'I have been watching the Six Nations rugby with the family. This has inspired the boys to get out the Duplo and build a rugby stadium. Hugo constructed the goals with great pride and Chris made the stadium.

The boys then watched an American sitcom where everybody trooped off to the baseball game. So out came the Duplo again and we then had a baseball stadium next to the rugby stadium. They used their Brio toy train to get the crowds from one stadium to the other.'

Inspire kids to perform

Use films and musicals as a source of ideas for kids to do their own performances. Agree a theme with the kids and help then find the appropriate costumes. Then leave them to it – but agree a time when you will come back to view the production.

'Emily likes Oliver the musical. So we've done a show of it. She'll copy the actions from the video.' *Julie, nanny of three kids*

Teresa says:

'Creating home videos of your children's productions can be a great way of inspiring them to put together something really good. This year the children have produced their own video and it was called 'The Tale Best not Told". They found a certificate on the front of an 18 video and some excellent graphics from the internet for the introductory frames. '

ACTIVITY DIARY – WEEK/DATE:

Chatter

Reading

Creativity/ music

Exercise

Home help

Play

Here's an Activity Diary to help you focus on the 6 ingredients. Use it to record any of the past week's activity highlights, or to plan the week ahead. Get a copy from www.mediadietforkids.com

Step 3 – summary

- Step 3 of The Media Diet is all about finding and encouraging media substitutes.
- It's all very well limiting screen entertainment time, but something positive needs to fill the void. We have all experienced that empty feeling after a period of media bingeing – some parents describe it as the 'cold turkey' moment.
- We believe that there are 6 ingredients that a parent should encourage when it's time to look beyond the screen – chat, reading, creativity and music, exercise, helping around the home ... .and above all, *play*.
- It's certainly worth investing time to get the balance right.

Conclusion — time to take action!

So, you've bought the book. You've read the diet. Now what?

The answer, of course, is to take action. And now's the time for a number of reasons.

For a start, there's no longer any doubt that too much time spent in front of the TV and computer can damage our children for life. It's a fact. It can. As parents, therefore, we should try and do what we can to limit and control our children's media consumption.

Once our children become teenagers we inevitably lose some control. We need, therefore, to establish good media habits in our kids at an early age, so that they can learn to take full responsibility for their own screen activity before their teenage years.

> 'Once you get over 12, it's hard to control. They've got to manage for themselves. It's important to set the parameters early. If you don't do that the cat is out of the bag.' *Kate, with two teenage kids*

> 'At 13 they may stay at home alone while you go out. As soon as you've gone out of the door you don't see what they're doing. And then they're off to friends so it's impossible to keep in touch with what they're doing.' *Elena, with son aged 13*

We also need to take action now because the task of controlling our kids' screen consumption is only going to get harder.

The media revolution is just beginning. Screens are becoming more and more part of our everyday lives. Large flat screens are turning our sitting rooms into private cinemas. And small portable screens are enabling us to do just about anything, anywhere. It's all great stuff, but the downside is that it makes it more difficult for us to control and monitor our children's screen consumption.

257

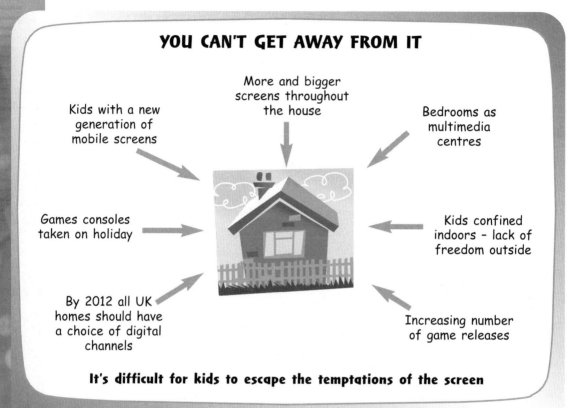

YOU CAN'T GET AWAY FROM IT

Kids with a new generation of mobile screens

More and bigger screens throughout the house

Bedrooms as multimedia centres

Games consoles taken on holiday

Kids confined indoors – lack of freedom outside

By 2012 all UK homes should have a choice of digital channels

Increasing number of game releases

It's difficult for kids to escape the temptations of the screen

If you let things get out of control, the consequences can be bad for everyone.

And, don't be put off from starting The Media Diet because you don't think you've got the time. The diet does require a little bit more time and effort from you as a parent, but probably not as much as you think. Once your child becomes less dependent on the screen, and better at entertaining his or herself, you'll get more of your own time back again.

The success of The Media Diet relies on you enthusing and involving your child right from the start. How you do it is up to you. We've tried to make it simple for you by including easy to read charts and illustrations throughout the book. Share – and enjoy – these pages with your child. Show them, for instance, The Media Clock (*see page 114*) and fill in The Media Time Check (*see page 119*) with them.

We all know the importance of looking left and right before we cross a road. The Media Diet for Kids is about instilling similar good habits in our children's approach to modern media. And if your kids cringe at the thought of it – as some of ours certainly did – try and find a family language, or particular way of doing things, to make it work. As we said earlier, it may help to think of the diet as a tool kit of ideas and thoughts. You can dip into it as you want. You may like some of the tools, but reject others. It doesn't matter. Have a go with them all and see which you prefer.

What's your family language?

As advertising and communication professionals, we naturally felt we wanted a slogan for The Media Diet. So, we turned to the people who matter the most – kids. What slogan would encourage them to take up the diet? What expression really hits the spot?

Well, not surprisingly, they all had different ideas. For Alice – aged 2 – it was as simple as 'Play now, telly later'. For Isabel – aged 12 – it was something more cool and modern – 'Go 4 Da Mix'. Some kids were turned on by the positive benefits they'd get from the diet, and others needed to be scared into action.

It made us think. Wouldn't it be better to let parents and children come up with their own family slogan? So, there's the challenge. Have fun and explore what language works best with you and your child.

You know you're winning when the kids take charge!

Most importantly, we hope we've given you the confidence to take action. We were struck by the number of parents we spoke to who had a niggling feeling that something wasn't quite right, but weren't sure whether or not they should take action – and, if they did do something, what it should be.

In fact, we were two such mums ourselves.

The Media Diet has helped us. But, remember it's a diet *for kids*. When you sense they are taking on responsibility for themselves, you know it's really working.

Let us know what family language you develop. And for more information and on-going discussion, go to www.mediadietforkids.com

Further food for thought

A selected menu of useful 'media websites'

1. Appropriate content

www.bbfc.co.uk
The British Board of Film Classification classifies films in the UK.

www.bfi.org.uk
The British Film Institute provides news and information on all types of films.

www.pegi.info
The Pan European Games Information (PEGI) is a new, pan-European age rating system for interactive games.

www.videostandards.org.uk
The Videos Standards Council provides advice to parents on videos and computer games.

2. Choosing computer games

www.pin.org.uk
The Parents' Information Network evaluates educational software and websites for kids.

www.brainworks.co.uk
An online brochure for fun, educational CD Roms, science discovery products and games.

3. Child-friendly search engines

www.askjeevesforkids.com

www.yahooligans.com

4. Internet safety

www.getnetwise.org

Offers detailed and comprehensive advice on all aspects of internet use, including information on filtering products. (Produced by internet companies and public interest groups.)

www.chatdanger.com

Outlines potential dangers of internet activity such as chat rooms and IM. Good site for parents to visit with kids. (Produced by Childnet International.)

www.fkbko.co.uk

Fun and easy to follow advice and information for kids on safe surfing. (Produced by For Kids by Kids Online.)

www.parentscentre.gov.uk

Comprehensive advice for parents on internet safety. (Produced by the Department of Education and Skills.)

www.thinkuknow.co.uk

Cartoon-based website with advice on safe internet surfing. (Produced by The Home Office.)

5. Media complaints and education

www.ofcom.org.uk

The Office of Communications (OFCOM) considers complaints about any TV or radio programme.

www.asa.org.uk
The Advertising Standards Authority considers complaints about TV or radio advertisements.

www.iwf.org.uk
The Internet Watch Foundation offers an authorized hotline for anyone to report illegal content on the internet.

www.mediasmart.org.uk
Media Smart helps kids understand and interpret advertising.

www.bbc.co.uk
The BBC runs an easy-to-follow Webwise Online Course. Great for parents who don't feel very internet-literate.

To find out details about popular children's websites and computer games, or for other media news and views, visit our website www.mediadietforkids.com

References

1. Youth TGI. Copyright BMRB International, 1994–2004.
2. Senate Judiciary Committee Staff Report, *Children, Violence and the Media*, 1999 (cited by TV-Turnoff Network, June 2005 (www.tvturnoff.org))
3. US News and World Report, 8 Apr 1997 (cited by TV-Turnoff Network, June 2005 (www.tvturnoff.org)).
4. BBC Radio 4, 23 Dec 2004.
5. Centrewall, BS 'Television and violence: the scale of the problem and where we go from here', *Journal of the American Medical Association*, vol. 267, 1992. Grossman, D and DeGaetano, G, *Stop teaching our kids to kill: a call to action against TV, movie and video game violence*, Random House, 1999. Killology Research Group (www.killology.com).
6. Teresa Orange Research, Nov 2004.
7. Browne, K and Hamilton-Giachritsis, C, 'The influence of violent media on children and adolescents: a public health approach', *The Lancet*, vol. 365, 19 Feb 2005.
8. Zimmerman, F, Glew, G, Christakis, D and Katon, W, 'Early cognitive stimulation, emotional support and television watching as predictors of subsequent bullying among grade-school children', *Archives of Pediatrics & Adolescent Medicine*, vol. 159, Apr 2005 (cited in 'Too much TV 'turns children into bullies', *Daily Telegraph,* 5 Apr 2005).
9. Coyne, SM, 'Indirect aggression on screen – a hidden problem?' *The Psychologist*, vol. 17, Dec 2004.
10. Robinson, T, Wilde, M, Navracruz, L, Haydel, F and Varady, A, 'Effects of reducing children's television and video game use on aggressive behaviour', *Archives of Pediatrics & Adolescent Medicine*, vol. 155, Jan 2001 (cited in 'Switching off TV cuts childhood aggression', *The Times,* 16 Jan 2001).
11. The Institute of Psychiatry, King's College, London, and the University of Manchester, 'Time trends in adolescent mental health', *Journal of Child Psychology and Psychiatry*, Nov 2004.
12. Livingstone, S and Bober, M, *UK Children Go Online*, July 2004 (www.children-go-online.net)
13. Office of Communications, *Childhood Obesity – Food Advertising in Context*, July 2004 (www.ofcom.org.uk)

14. Salti, R, Meyer Hospital, University of Florence (cited in 'Watching TV may speed up puberty', *BBC News*, 28 June 2004).

15. World Health Organization, 'Sedentary lifestyle: a global public health problem', June 2005 (www.who.int).

16. A report from the Chief Medical Officer, *At least five a week – evidence of the impact of physical activity and its relationship to health*, Apr 2004.

17. Hancox, R, Milne, B and Poulton, R, 'Association between child and adolescent television viewing and adult health: a longitudinal birth cohort study', *The Lancet*, vol. 364, 17 July 2004.

18. Dr Faisel Khan, Dundee University (cited in 'One in five teenagers show signs of heart disease', *Daily Telegraph*, 7 Sept 2004).

19. Harvard School of Public Health, June 1999 (cited in TV-Turnoff Network, June 2005 (www.tvturnoff.org)).

20. Weikart, PS, *Round the Circle: Key Experiences in Movement for Young Children* (cited in Lodge, M, *Set Free Childhood*, Hawthorn Press, 2003).

21. The British Chiropratic Association, press release, 1 Sept 2004 (www.chiropractic-uk.co.uk).

22. PRIO Corporation, press release, 6 Mar 2001 (www.prio.com).

23. 'Don't allow under-9's to use a mobile', *Daily Telegraph*, 12 Jan 2005.

24. National Center for Educational Statistics, 1990. Nation's Report Card 1990. National Center for Educational Statistics, 2000. Fourth-Grade Reading 2000 (cited by TV-Turnoff Network, June 2005 (www.tvturnoff.org)).

25. Christakis, D, Zimmerman, F, Di Giuseppe, D and McCarty, C, 'Early Television Exposure and Subsequent Attentional Problems in Children', *Pediatrics*, vol. 113, Apr 2004.

26. Wilson, G, University of London (cited in 'Texting and emailing "fog your brain like cannabis"', *Daily Mail*, 22 Apr 2005).

27. The Broadcasting Standards Commission and The Independent Television Commission, *What Children Watch*, June 2003.

28. Close, R, *Television and language development in the early years: a review of the literature*, Mar 2004.

29. Duffy L, Fox F, Horwood H, Northstone K and the ALSPAC Study team, 'Can television viewing habits affect language development in young children?' *Literacy Today*, vol. 39, June 2004.

30. The Basic Skills Agency, *Survey into Children's Skills on Entry into Education*, 2005 (www.basic-skills-wales.org).

31. www.literacytrust.org.uk/Researcherindex/SallyWard.html.

32. National Center for Educational Statistics, 2000 (cited by TV-Turnoff Network, June 2005 (www.tvturnoff.org)).

33. The Levinson Medical Center for Learning Disabilities, (www.dyslexiaonline.com) (cited in 'Girl who beat dyslexia with tablets for travel-sick spacemen', *Daily Mail*, 28 Dec 2000).

34. Healy, J, *Failure to Connect: How computers affect our children's minds – for better and worse*, Simon & Schuster, New York, 1998 (cited in Lodge, M, *Set Free Childhood*, Hawthorn Press, 2003.

35. 'Parents criticized for sending children to school "half asleep"', *Daily Telegraph*, 4 May 2004.

36. University of Oxford (cited in 'Today's couch potatoes are tomorrow's insomniacs', *Daily Mail*, 14 June 2004).

37. Johnson, J, Dr, Columbia University, New York (cited in 'Today's couch potatoes are tomorrow's insomniacs', *Daily Mail*, 14 June 2004).

38. 'Lonely future predicted for the PlayStation children', *The Times*, 29 Oct 2004.

39. 'One in four under-eights have a mobile', *Daily Mail*, 15 Feb 2005.

40. Mintel, *Marketing to 11–14 year olds, April 2004*; *Toy retailing in the UK*, Apr 2004.

41. The Guide Association, Feb 2002 (cited by National Literacy Trust (www.literacytrust.org.uk)).

42. Haste, H, University of Bath/Mori/Nestle Social Research Programme (cited in 'Don't speak, text, says mobile generation', *Daily Telegraph*, 20 Dec 2004).

43. South West Learning and Skills Council, Jan 2004 (cited by National Literacy Trust (www.literacytrust.org.uk)).

44. American Academy of Pediatrics 'Children and Advertising' Factsheet, 2002 (cited by TV-Turnoff Network, June 2005 (www.tvturnoff.org)).

45. Livingstone, S and Bovill, M, *Young People New Media*, London School of Economics and Political Science, 1999.

46. American Academy of Pediatrics (www.aap.org)

47. *Health Survey for England 2002 – The Health of Children and Young People. The Scottish Health Survey 1998.*

Index

We hope you enjoyed this Hay House book.
If you would like to receive a free catalogue featuring additional
Hay House books and products, or if you would like information
about the Hay Foundation, please contact:

Hay House UK Ltd

Unit 62, Canalot Studios • 222 Kensal Rd • London W10 5BN
Tel: (44) 20 8962 1230; Fax: (44) 20 8962 1239
www.hayhouse.co.uk

***

Published and distributed in the United States of America by:
Hay House, Inc. • PO Box 5100 • Carlsbad, CA 92018-5100
Tel: (1) 760 431 7695 or (800) 654 5126;
Fax: (1) 760 431 6948 or (800) 650 5115
www.hayhouse.com

Published and distributed in Australia by:
Hay House Australia Ltd • 18/36 Ralph St • Alexandria NSW 2015
Tel: (61) 2 9669 4299 • Fax: (61) 2 9669 4144
www.hayhouse.com.au

Published and distributed in the Republic of South Africa by:
Hay House SA (Pty) Ltd • PO Box 990 • Witkoppen 2068
Tel/Fax: (27) 11 706 6612 • orders@psdprom.co.za

Distributed in Canada by:
Raincoast • 9050 Shaughnessy St • Vancouver, BC V6P 6E5
Tel: (1) 604 323 7100 • Fax: (1) 604 323 2600

***

Sign up via the Hay House UK website to receive the Hay House
online newsletter and stay informed about what's going on with
your favourite authors. You'll receive bimonthly announcements
about discounts and offers, special events, product highlights,
free excerpts, giveaways, and more!
www.hayhouse.co.uk